W9-BOM-318

Teachers' Voices:
Portfolios in the Classroom

KBBreece
Sept 1994

TEACHERS' VOICES
Portfolios in the Classroom

Mary Ann Smith
Miriam Ylvisaker
editors

Berkeley
National Writing Project
1993

National Writing Project Corporation
Copyright © 1993
All Rights Reserved.
Printed in the United States of America.
No part of this book may be used or reproduced in any manner
whatsoever without written permission, except in the case of
brief quotations used in critical articles or reviews.
Please direct reprinting requests and book orders to:

National Writing Project, Graduate School of Education,
615 University Hall, University of California,
Berkeley, CA 94720.
Telephone 510-642-0963
Fax 510-642-4545

Library of Congress Cataloging-in-Publication Data

Teachers' voices: portfolios in the classroom / Mary Ann Smith,
Miriam Ylvisaker, editors.
p.   cm.
Includes bibliographical references.
ISBN: 1-883920-07-08
!. Portfolios in education.   I. Smith, Mary Ann, 1942-
II. Ylvisaker, Miriam
LB 1029.P67T43   1993
371. 3'078--dc20   93-5274

Cover design by Dennis Teutschel

Foreword

This book represents the continuing commitment of the National Writing Project to the belief that teachers of writing must write themselves. It is only through the experience of writing that the process becomes familiar; it is only then that teachers can understand the difficulties students encounter and can find ways to help them over writing hurdles. Both teachers and students experience a sense of satisfaction and excitement when they produce an excellent piece of writing. For teachers, their own writing becomes a source of rejuvenation both in and out of the classroom.

This book, which is the first in the newly-resumed National Writing Project publications series, talks about ways teachers have found to move student writing from piece-by-piece accumulation to what represents, for each student, a unique body of work. In this small volume, thirteen outstanding teachers think through for us the virtues and pitfalls of portfolio-keeping, tussling with ideas about how and why a portfolio adds dimensions to classroom writing and evaluation. Here we have descriptions of how teachers have changed the ways they work with students and with each other, and we have a delineation of that step in the writing process often skimped or overlooked — the reflectiveness that allows the writer to move from good to better and beyond. Here we have writing and thinking inextricably linked in strong teachers' voices that inform us and inform the profession.

James Gray
Director, National Writing Project

Table of Contents

Introduction:
Portfolio Classrooms

Mary Ann Smith

This is not a book about right answers. It's a book about thinking. It's a book that announces on every page that the value of creating portfolios is in the thinking it asks of both students and teachers.

Fortunately, thinking is back in fashion. Students are problem-solving and conceptualizing in mathematics; hypothesizing and proving in science; making applications in history. Whether or not thinking is prefaced by the word "critical" and however it is defined in a particular discipline, it has regained its place as a desirable means and end in a good education.

As this book testifies, students are thinking not only about mathematics, science, or history, but also about their own learning. Portfolios give students the wide angle and the zoom lens by which to view and present themselves as learners, thinkers, and writers. In the process of creating portfolios, they spread out their writing, analyze and revise it, present it encased in more writing that explains how it came to be and what its special strengths are. In other words, students engage in activities that promote learning while becoming more perceptive about that learning.

Teachers, too, use the process of creating portfolios for learning and thinking about their work. They analyze and revise what happens in the classroom. In fact, this book moves into such classrooms, allowing us to watch the teachers as they make and discard decisions, replay the results of this or that teaching strategy, and study their students closely. The book does exactly what Ed Reidy of the Kentucky Department of Education insists is important to any investigation of portfolios: it offers portfolios of portfolio journeys. It records risks and blind alleys, as well as successes. It records what happens in real classrooms.

Notable in these classrooms is the lack of anti-thinking devices, the kinds of packages and kits that litter much of today's educational turf. The teachers' message is that the price of purchased decisions is too high. There is no substitute for learning to make your own. If we are to have a "thinking" curriculum in education, as David and Lauren Resnick call it, then we cannot market it as prepackaged materials.

However, even portfolios cannot guarantee thinking. As Catharine Lucas points out, portfolios can actually constrain a classroom:

> *To the extent that the tasks included in the portfolio are narrowly set and standardized, to reduce the 'messiness' of the data and make performance more comparable from student to student, the portfolio will, like other external tests before it, dictate rather than reflect curriculum. And to the extent that the pieces collected are written 'for the test' rather than for the learners and their audiences, the opportunities for students to engage in purposeful task definition, reflection, and self-evaluation will be truncated.*

The argument, then, is to let portfolios be internal and meaningful and nested in the thinking of those who actually live and work in classrooms. This book is a testimony to that argument, to thinking professionals, and to the profession itself.

The pages ahead dispel some myths and uncover some facts about portfolios.

Portfolios come in all shapes and sizes and styles ...

The thirteen teachers in this book have tailored portfolios to their students and to their own best teaching practices. Dixie Dellinger, in "Portfolios: A Personal History," illustrates how portfolios have grown out of and reinforced what she regards as pivotal teaching and learning strategies in her North Carolina classroom. While ready-to-wear portfolios are increasingly available, teachers like Dellinger question or avoid them altogether. The commonly-held belief seems to be that portfolios contribute the most to learning when they are "under-invented," that is, when they ask more and more of students. In fact, these teachers are replacing the devices that students have too often coasted on: paint-by-number requirements that represent someone else's thinking. Instead, these teachers offer support for students to do their own thinking. These teachers also resist enroachment on the individual character of portfolios in their classrooms. Fern Tavalin, in "Vermont Writing Portfolios," points out the mischief that occurs when state testing agencies, regardless of good intentions, "think" for the students about portfolio contents and contexts.

Portfolios thrive or starve, depending on the classroom ...

First, portfolios depend on classrooms that offer certain kinds of activities. For example, in portfolio classrooms, reading and writing and talking are everyday occurrences. Revising and reflecting are regular events, highly valued and frequently practiced. Some call this kind of classroom a "learning community." Some call it an "interactive classroom." Whatever the label, the environment supports students as they mull over and build on what they know. For Joni Chancer ("The Teacher's Role in Portfolio Assessment"), the teacher is the essential designer of this environment, the person who sets in motion the mini-lessons, conversations, writing workshops, book clubs — in short, the culture that nourishes portfolios.

The second feature of a portfolio classroom is that it fosters partnerships among students and teachers. Everyone is cast in the role of learner. Everyone shares joint responsibility — and enjoyment — for decisions and demands. The teachers in this book refer constantly to the give-and-take that goes on in their classrooms. They remind us that we see more when we compare notes about what we have seen. I have a friend who is farsighted while I am nearsighted. Together, we say, we have perfect eyesight. So it is here. It takes both teachers and students to see and benefit from the making of a portfolio. In "Listening to Gia," Susan Reed shows us how a single student can sharpen a teacher's view of the way all students approach writing, response groups, reflection, and other learning events in a portfolio classroom.

Portfolios are like writing itself ...

Like writing, they have different purposes. We encounter a range here: portfolios for the purposes of showing off the best, demonstrating progress, presenting the drafts and decisions that go into a piece of writing, assembling the reach of a writer's learning. In fact, the success of portfolios as a teaching and learning tool seems to lie, in part, on how clearly teachers and students understand and agree on purposes. Nancy Green, in "Portfolios in a Fifth Grade Classroom," demonstrates that the purposes for portfolios actually guide other decisions and negotiations that pop up as classroom residents begin to live with portfolios.

Like writing, portfolios also have audiences. The teachers in this book have found multiple audiences for portfolios, including themselves, students, parents, other teachers, administrators, neighbors, and student-selected "outsiders." Again, audiences strongly influence the results of portfolio projects. What students select and how they present their work can certainly depend on who receives it. In "A First Grade Perspective," Lois Brandts talks about involving families from the outset, finding that their participation in the portfolio process brings home and school together and makes the portfolio more meaningful.

Like writing, portfolios involve processes. On one level, portfolios extend the time devoted to writing and its many stages. Teachers, like those we meet here, invite their students to return over and over again to what they have written, to re-see and revise and recall their thinking along the way. In other words, a student writer is not completely restrained by time or "teaching unit" or discrete assignment. On another level, teachers use portfolios to help students examine the processes that work best for them and to examine the changing nature of those processes. Whereas "the writing process" has been standardized and trivialized by publishers and other well-meaning outsiders, those on the inside of portfolio work demonstrate that the way writers write varies from writer to writer, from piece to piece, and from year to year. One insider, Jane Juska, also shows us, with tongue hovering near cheek ("No More One-Shots"), that students can manipulate processes in ways yet to be imagined and that their countless drafts can become unrelenting reminders of what happens when processes are unleashed.

Portfolios shift more authority to the student ...

As this book makes clear, most teachers have asked students to take charge of their portfolios. The thinking seems to be that students, if they are owners of their work, will behave like owners. They will be proud and conscientious and responsible. As they make and justify their portfolio choices, they will come to terms with the quality of those choices. They will look to themselves, rather than always to the teacher, for judgments about their strengths and limitations as writers. They will chart progress and set new goals for themselves. It is clear that students would learn considerably less if they were denied any of these experiences, if they were simply handed a blueprint for their portfolios. On the other hand, teachers here note with some humor that students, once they wake up from their school-induced comas, are full of surprises. They may, for a time, become more dependent. They may make disappointing choices for even more disappointing reasons. Becoming an authority — particularly if one has never had the pleasure — is sometimes a bumpy passage. In "Casting My Net," Tamsie West notes that even Mississippi's finest Advanced Placement students can fluctuate between cooperative and cranky on the road to self-evaluation.

Portfolios are close encounters of the right kind ...

When students and teachers have to "cover" curriculum, give and receive "points," rank and be ranked, they have little opportunity to know and appreciate each other as learners and as human beings. The teachers here frequently mention that portfolios help them understand their students in some new way. After all, portfolios provide a whole array of pictures, with captions and commentary, that expand the view of an individual, rather than distort and diminish the individual on the basis of a single event or worse yet, a single score. Mary Kay Deen's "Portfolios as Discovery" recalls her own experiences with school tests that narrowly defined her and contrasts those tests with portfolios that have allowed her primary students to shine.

Portfolios can also stir up conversations among teachers. Typically, the school culture promotes professional distance. Instead of inviting teachers to watch each other teach, to debate best practices, to pool resources, the culture walls off teachers and parcels out their time. School often looks like the sandbox Piaget describes in which small children play side-by-side but not together. But where teachers have joined forces to experiment with portfolios, they have been able to change the nature of the sandbox. In "An English Department Portfolio Project," Jan Bergamini describes a four-year English department portfolio venture during which her faculty became a community of learners.

Portfolios mark the growth of students and other notables ...

One of the key markers of a portfolio environment is momentum. Students not only make strides, they account for those strides, so that their learning becomes conscious and retrievable. For example, they articulate which writing strategies they have added to their repertoires. In this way, they can call on these strategies, draw from their personal bank accounts whenever they sit down to write. They no longer have to depend solely on some kind of happy accident to make their writing successful. The idea of tracking growth and creating momentum simply means treating what is being learned — with all the detours that come up in any student's development — as more important than some isolated effort.

When teachers focus on individual progress, they can keep their curricula and assessments moving forward, responsive to growth. They can "up the ante," offering new challenges or directions. How different from hand-me-down curricula that never grow with the students and teachers. How different from the standard, plain-brown-wrapper assessment whose contents guarantee an annual misery of sameness.

The era of shedding wrappers and generic tasks seems to be here. With portfolios, classroom work can be open to view and to improvements all year long. The portfolios themselves can be refined at any time. The taboos of the past, taboos that kept teachers and students from reconceiving their efforts are now in question. In their account of a Virginia English department portfolio project, "Interviewing Students About Their Portfolios," Bob Ingalls and Joyce Jones show us how the teachers dipped back into their assessment to improve it and how they involved students in studying the evolution of the assessment and of their own writing.

Portfolios take us behind-the-scenes ...

With portfolios, students ask themselves tough questions: Which pieces of writing best represent me as a writer? What do I mean by good writing? How will I present these writings to my readers? What was difficult or irritating or easy about this writing? What were the turning points or discoveries? What have I learned about writing and the processes I use to write? In other words, students are invited to tell the story behind the stories they have written.

Most important, they are no longer confined to a single assignment. Instead, they can see the entire landscape of their work. And through reflection, they can give meaning and perspective to the landscape. In fact, as John Dorroh demonstrates in "Portfolios in Biology," students can investigate their learning in any discipline.

So what?

Clearly, portfolios are important in themselves. But they are also symbolic of the growth in teacher professionalism and classroom practice that has been under way ever since the National Writing Project began twenty years ago. Over this time, NWP teachers have constructed an ever-elastic body of knowledge and a professional community that continually stretches that knowledge, testing it against new students and new situations and new discoveries. The fact that successful portfolio practices have emerged from such a community is not surprising in the least.

Yet teachers are always being pulled in opposing directions. At the same time they are authoring assessments that are responsive and challenging to their students, many are also administering institutional assessments. At the same time that teachers are experimenting with what it means to evaluate students in the context of individual development, they are handed definitive scores for these students, scores that sort students into predetermined and relative categories. Teachers live in a crossfire between external demands and the demands that emerge from their own reflective practice.

One reason, then, that teachers participate year after year in a professional community is to sustain and expand what they know, lest it be lost in a trend toward standardized or mandated reforms. Many of the teachers writing in this book collaborated systematically with Writing Project colleagues on developing classroom portfolios. Tamsie West, for one, credits her portfolio response group with pointing out that "in these portfolios I had physical proof of the kind of teaching that had gone on in my classroom, that I could show that the method I had used to teach had made a significant difference in students' writing abilities and maturity levels." John Dorroh says that "After my first meeting with the [Writing Project] task force in October, I had a much clearer ideas of how portfolios could be used in my science class." Lois Brandts' portfolio research group was a source of "hilarity and truth." Jane Juska took her portfolio problems over the phone line to Susan Reed.

In a larger context, the sustained involvement of teachers in Writing Project communities provides them with support to sustain a similar community within their own classrooms. As learners, researchers, and authors, these teachers "understand experientially what it means to construct knowledge in a community of learners and will devote themselves to figuring out how to turn their own classrooms into such communities for their students. They need — we all need — to continually renew and deepen our sense of what such a community is and feels like because it is so easy to forget and so difficult to replicate in classrooms."

The "so what?" of portfolios, then, is precisely this: Portfolios are the concrete embodiment of the substantial strategies National Writing Project teachers are using in their classrooms, of the professional community to which they belong, and of the community they have established with their students. In the hands of these teachers, portfolios are more than just portfolios. They are another step in a reform movement that continues to improve student writing, to promote teacher inquiry and to prove the wisdom of NWP founder and director James Gray, who insists on this principle: Teachers are the best teachers of other teachers.

References

Blau, S. (1993). Constructing knowledge in a professional community: The writing project as a model for classrooms. *The NWP/CSW Quarterly, 15* (1), 16-19.

Lucas, C. (1992). Introduction: Writing portfolios—changes and challenges. In K. B. Yancey (Ed.). *Portfolios in the writing classroom.* Urbana, IL: National Council of Teachers of English.

Piaget, J. (1960) *The child's conception of physical causality.* Gabain, J., tr. Paterson, NJ: Littlefield, Adams.

Reidy, E. (1993). Address to the California Learning Assessment System Portfolio Task Force. Sacramento, CA.

Resnick, D. & Resnick, L. (1990) Setting a new standard: Toward an examination system for the United States. Unpublished proposal. Pittsburgh: University of Pittsburgh, Learning Research and Development Center, National Center on Education and the Economy.

Portfolios: A Personal History

Dixie Dellinger

A North Carolina teacher has been experimenting with portfolios of one kind or another for thirteen years. She looks at each experiment in terms of what it asks of her students and how it reflects a new stage in her teaching.

Portfolios are currently generating great interest around the country. A body of literature about them is growing, teachers are curious about them, and efforts are increasing to use them on a large scale to improve assessment. Some of the nation's leading school systems are undertaking and even mandating portfolio projects. The word "portfolio" is becoming wedded to "assessment," as in the song about love and marriage — "You can't have one without the other."

However, just as love and marriage can be considered separately, so portfolios can be considered apart from assessment. Even though portfolios can be more revealing of real learning than traditional assessment measures, they can have other important purposes as well. Perhaps the story of my own use of portfolios can draw attention to some of those other purposes.

The value of collecting work and putting it into some kind of format for presenting to others or to one's self was uppermost in my mind in the early 80s when I first asked my students to assemble what is now called a "portfolio." I did not use the word "portfolio" then, because I had not thought of it nor had I read anything about it. I did have some idea of assessment in mind, but I had in mind more the idea of a showcase. (I'm sure I used that exact word.) Later, when I first began to ask my students to assemble "portfolios," I still didn't ask myself what a portfolio was "supposed" to be and I didn't look anywhere to find out. It was whatever the students and I made it, and it still is.

My own experience with portfolios evolved as a natural outgrowth of changed teaching in my classroom. After working with the National Writing Project in 1980, I began to teach writing as process. I was also working out sequenced writing assignments according to James Moffett's theories (*Teaching the Universe of Discourse*, 1968). I have told that story elsewhere (*Out of the Heart*, 1982). These assignments led to increased quantities and to greater varieties of writing, and required my ideas about assessing and grading writing to change. My students — eleventh and twelfth graders of all ability levels — and I were becoming increasingly accustomed to writing without the papers being graded, and the students were taking much more pride in their work. In our curriculum at that time we had semester courses in composition, and writing folders became very thick by the end of the course. Some analyzing and summarizing needed to be done in order to make meaning of the total body of work, both for my students and myself.

For me, the idea of what later became portfolios in my classroom was preceded by the practice of doing an inventory, which I learned from Dixie Goswami in 1982. This process, a natural fit with those thick folders, involved assembling all the work in the writing folder, arranging it in chronological order, and then completing a three-columned analysis or inventory. In column one, the student listed each piece, in column two, she described the piece, and in column three, she commented in some way upon the piece. This inventory was turned in with the writing folder for a major part of the final grade, and I responded to column three, commending good insights and thoughtful comments.

The inventory encouraged students to keep everything they wrote and to analyze the total body of their work during the course, rather than to focus on isolated papers or on grade averages. Frequent comments were, "I can't believe I wrote all this!" and "I didn't realize I was learning so much!" Thus, the inventory proved to be a highly effective tool for meta-analysis and metacognition and led to a totally different attitude toward a semester's school work. Without consciously knowing it, I had moved both myself and my students into a growth model of learning, at least as far as composition was concerned.

During the first year that my students did these inventories, I saw them making such comments as "I like this piece best of all," or "I am proud that I learned to do this," or "I think I used very good description here," or "The best part of this one is the ending." So there seemed to be a need for something more than the inventory and our videotaped final Read-A-Round. Students were doing so much good writing that it craved some kind of celebration with permanency. It seemed to me that the writer should be the one to select what she wanted to celebrate and for what reason, and that idea brought up what I now call a portfolio.

The portfolio concept originated with the visual arts. We have seen artists dashing about the streets in New York with their large leather portfolios, seeking jobs or arranging for gallery showings. The portfolio, a collection of works selected and ordered by the "author," represents a selection governed by some purpose; the preparer often includes some explanatory material to set the context.

So my first uses of the portfolio concept came when I asked students — after completing their inventories — to make books of their best writing, to include their own choice of examples of the kinds of writing we had been learning to do, along with a "free choice" favorite, to design an original cover, make a table of contents, and write a dedication and a preface in which they acknowledged help they had received. We had begun the course by interviewing each other and writing personality profiles, so we used these as "author blurbs" on the back covers. Then, each student chose a piece from her book to read in the final Read-A-Round, introducing herself and telling a bit about how the piece was conceived and written. I still have those videos and treasure

13

them. I laminated all the book covers, and each student took home with great pride a collection of his or her best work. I didn't grade these books; I simply wrote a brief positive comment about what I saw in each one: versatility, fluency, commitment, and so on. We didn't call this a portfolio; we just called it a book.

Here is an excerpt from the general letter I included in each book when it was returned to the student, showing my thinking about writing and learning at that time:

> *Almost all of you learned some new things and almost all of you got something done that you were proud of. The books show that. Many of the books are incredibly fine and sincere, coming right from the heart of students who really have learned that writing is not 'just old school work' but something real that is part of life. Those books are not always the ones that have everything spelled right or all the grammar correct. They are the ones put together with the kind of care that shows their authors cared about their writing — not simply their grade. For the rest of their lives, these people will write with a different feeling about it, and I think they will read what other people write with a different feeling, too. That's 'education' of the best kind! Congratulations!!*

At about the same time, I was introduced to reader-response critical theory and a write-while-you-read process for using it. "Writing to learn," as I called it, quickly became the core of my instructional methods in literature studies, replacing the structured analytical note-taking I had formerly required. Again, this produced much more writing of a kind that obviously should not be graded piece by piece. After a time of accumulating rich, thick reading-response journals, I again felt a great need for some reflection, analysis, and selectivity, as well as celebration.

In a semester course in European literature, I asked the students to do an inventory of all their work and then select three best examples, either from reading-response journals or compositions, and bind these with the inventory. To this, I added the final exam essays and gave the whole packet a large part of the semester grade. It seemed a much more effective way of evaluating what the students had learned by reading and writing. We still didn't call this a portfolio, though.

In another course on American dialects later that year, the students put together a collection of work from papers, presentations, and projects. I evaluated that collection as a major part of final grades, based on what it showed about students' learning in the subject and their carefulness with dialectal field work. This time I gave it the name "portfolio," and the second-semester composition students called their book a "portfolio" also.

So that is how I started, around ten years ago. Since those early beginnings I have come to make the concept of portfolio an integral part of my classes. I use the concept in a variety of ways, some of which figure into my assessment methods and some of which serve only to foster the students' self-assessment.

How do I introduce the concept of a portfolio? At some points it is good just to stop and take stock. I may take a class period sometime in October and say, "Go through your writing folder and choose the three pieces you like best and write something about why you like them and how you came to write them. Put all this in another folder, date it and save it." Or I may say, "Go through your reading-response journal and select the five best pages and write something about what they show of you as a reader and thinker. Date this and save it." I always read these very carefully, but I do not grade them. This act of choosing introduces the students to the idea that the judgment of what is best is their own and that they need to share the reasons for that choice with their reader.

This act of choosing also establishes a personal ownership of school experience that is too often precluded by usual classroom methods. Indeed, if I have already put any kind of marks on pieces in the folder, I find the students simply choosing their "bests" on the basis of those marks. One eleventh-grade boy put it this way:

I feel that I've grown in my reading, thinking, and writing. At the begin of the year in my journals I made check minuses, but later in the year I began to make checks and check pluses.

Such is the power of external assessment to displace self-analysis.

An early ungraded introduction of the portfolio concept has many other benefits. It encourages a long-range view of learning, something "low-ability" students are hardly ever asked to take, evidenced by the fact that they rarely keep their work and sometimes have never learned or cared to keep up with a notebook or folder. If they haven't begun to keep things, this gives them a good reason to do so, without imposing a grade penalty. Thereafter, when I say, "Never throw anything away," they know that I mean it — and why. Keeping and organizing one's work, seemingly a mundane matter, is a crucial factor in academic success. It is, of course, only one step from there to reflection, the beginning of higher-order thinking. Yet, it is a giant leap forward from the fragmented, particle-based "teach-test-forget" structures so often used. A portfolio of the simplest sort can accomplish this vital step, and it does not need to be graded. In fact, I think if I graded at this point, it would short-circuit the entire reflective process.

Preparing this initial portfolio encourages a student to appreciate herself and make a commitment to her education. Reading what has been written earlier creates a sense of confidence and pride, as I noticed in the inventory process. I often hear someone say while going through the folder or the notebook, "I really like this. I had forgotten I wrote it," or "I really got into that piece of reading; it made me think. This is a good journal. I'll put it in." If we want students to learn, they must first become engaged in the process and in the classroom. A reflective student is an engaged learner. Without portfolios, getting that engagement is often difficult.

These short pauses to select work for a portfolio increase engagement and motivation and de-emphasize grades. Of course, what the student selects may not always be her best work; it will be what she chooses for her own reasons, such as this comment I read last year: "I chose my piece about my grandmother because I love her so much, and this piece shows that." Had I been selecting, I would not have chosen that piece because it was all direct statements without much detail and I, as reader, did not feel that I knew the grandmother from the writing. Without the comment from the student, I would never have known the emotional investment she had made in that piece. As teacher, I need to remember that I am not the sole and ultimate judge of what is good in a student's work, that my criteria are not the only criteria, that writers own their writing, and that students own their lives. This initial portfolio helps me to keep that in mind.

Working on that first portfolio in class also brings the learning group's ideas together. One will say to another, "I think you ought to choose your piece about your accident. It makes me feel like I was there." Occasionally a student will write in her commentary, "I included this piece because my group really likes it." In this way, a community of writers begins to take shape.

After this beginning, I always ask the students to prepare a portfolio at the end of the semester and again at the end of the year, and I use them for various purposes — often as a part of the grade but more often for the activity itself. It all depends on our objectives.

Here is the preface that Heather, a junior, wrote in her portfolio:

> *Dear reader,*
>
> *'My Verdict' and 'A Poem' are the two pieces of writing that I have chosen to demonstrate my best qualities as a student and a writer. 'My Verdict' is my own personal opinion of the innocence of the person in question during the Salem witch trials. This paper reveals my best qualities as a student through the structure of sentences and paragraphs in the paper. I was taught the proper way of writing a paper of opinion (this includes an 'although' sentence, presenting the opposing side, presenting my side, and the conclusion) and I used it correctly through this piece. My abilities as a writer are shown through the smoothness of the paper...*

About her selection, "A Poem," Heather said:

> *As a student, I have learned to apply personification and metaphors in my work. 'A Poem' demonstrates this through*

the use of metaphor and personification and through the smoothness of its reading.

I was interested to note that Heather made a fine distinction between features; she had learned persuasive forms and poetic devices as a student but she had produced the "smoothness"" from her own ability as a writer. I appreciated the nice balance she saw between what I was teaching her and what she contributed from her own ability.

My response to her portfolio was:

Dear Heather,

From reading your folder, I can see that you are a careful and thoughtful writer who wants her work to be honest and vivid. You can look back at your work and evaluate it objectively, and you know when you have it the way you want it. You try the things you learn and work at getting the best possible word.

When portfolios are geared toward specific content objectives, I may prescribe the number and types of items the student is to include in her portfolio, such as the best piece of narrative, of exposition, or persuasion, and so on. These portfolios can be collected at any point in a course and used to assess mastery and/or to plan for further instruction. This was part of my original intent in that composition course ten years ago when the folders had grown so fat.

On the other hand, I often say now, "Select up to ten exhibits, limit twenty-five total pages, that will show you as a reader, a writer, and a thinker to someone else [not me] who would read your portfolio. Write a commentary that says what each piece demonstrates." Such were my instructions for the end-of-year portfolio in Advanced English III this past year.

In her end-of-year portfolio, Heather said,

In my responses to 'Those Winter Sundays,' Huckleberry Finn, *and* The Scarlet Letter, *I feel that I brought out a lot of ideas and a lot of possibilities of how the author and the characters felt. This work displays my ability to read and comprehend what I am reading. It has helped me tremendously to write these responses because it has given me a chance to develop an opinion and come to terms with how I felt about what I read.*

She goes on to review her selections and later comments on her ability as a writer:

Henry David Thoreau inspired me to write 'A Day of Solitude' upon reading Walden. *Again, I feel my ability as a writer shows through my choice of words and especially my sentence structure, which I feel is like Thoreau's.*

She included a free-writing done when reading Emerson:

As we read an excerpt out of Emerson's 'Self-Reliance,' I found myself in agreement with most of the points and it really made me stop and think. I like to think about the same things Emerson thinks about and thoroughly enjoyed reading this. My response ... was just a kind of opening for me and then I really got into all these thoughts that had been in my mind but never proposed to me. After I got into it is when I wrote 'Non-Conformity.' I did not try to advance my ability as a writer in any way in this. It was ... a free-writing ... This piece displays me as a thinker. That was the whole purpose of writing it. This was just something I did to develop my thoughts. I turned it in just to see what someone who is fluent with Emerson and these ideas would think.

Heather also included the same poem she had chosen at mid-year, but now she has this to say about it:

'A Poem' is one of my favorites also. I like all the ideas but it is definitely not in its finished form.

19

She had revised it twice during this year.

In all the flexibility and variety that is possible with classroom portfolios, two things seem essential: the student selects and orders the exhibits according to some specific purpose; the student does some analysis and reflection that is made known to the reader.

From a teacher's point of view, there are several important reasons for creating a portfolio, some of which are indicated in what I have described. (See opposite page.)

At this time, I see four major reasons for portfolio use:

If we adopt the growth model of learning/teaching, then a portfolio approach is natural ...

We would ask students to assemble a "How I'm Growing" portfolio intended to show growth over time. It would contain works from beginning to present, including all types of work. Not all would be the best, nor would the student necessarily show equal growth in all aspects of learning. The purpose is exactly what it says: to observe learning and to observe growth, and the student should be growing also in her ability to observe and to assess that growth.

However, it has been my experience that a growth portfolio is difficult for a student to assemble effectively, except in specific matters, such as ability to use easily identifiable mechanical techniques. Much growth in learning occurs in ways that are only indirectly observable; much evidence of growth in samples is inferential. What one evaluator might see as growth, another might miss.

If we are working with our students in a growth model of learning we need portfolios, but we need to be wary of how we use them for assessment. It is touchy to ask a student to assemble a portfolio to show growth and then base formal assessments on it, for if the student's conclusions differ from the evaluator's, the student will lose faith in his ability to choose well or to reflect upon his work. Whenever I ask students to assemble growth portfolios, I respect their assessments, adding only comments that call attention to growth they might not have recognized.

THE PORTFOLIO — MORE THAN ASSESSMENT	
Increases quantity of writing	Increases writing by encouraging student involvement Lessens the "paper load"
Improves quality of learning	Encourages growth over time rather than "bead-stringing" Values each stage of growth (including notes, drafts, and revisions)
Contributes to cognitive growth	Encourages students to describe and analyze rather than judge, to evaluate and support with evidence, and to reflect over time
Undergirds curricular goals	Reinforces learning objectives and activities; serves as basis for making individual plans; teaches discrete skills
Serves as credential	Demonstrates skills, techniques, and practices, predicts potential, and opens lines of communication between high school and college
PORTFOLIOS CELEBRATE ACHIEVEMENT AND LEARNING	

If we adopt a process model of teaching/learning, then a portfolio will enhance it ...

We would ask the students to assemble a "How I Function" portfolio, intended to examine process. This one would include drafts, notes, composing diaries or protocols, reading-response journals, analyses, or commentaries. Again, these will not necessarily be only the best; the goal is to analyze one's processes, whether or not successful. This is not limited to writing processes, but can also illuminate reading processes, study processes, research or investigation processes, or — with very sophisticated students — thinking and reasoning processes. Such a portfolio becomes useful in teaching and assessing processes and can become a guide for future instruction.

If we want to adopt essential principles of mastery learning, a portfolio is essential ...

We would ask the students to assemble a "What I Can Do" portfolio. This portfolio would include exhibits selected according to what has been taught. The student's accompanying reflection should state how she sees these masteries connected to each other. This portfolio has an advantage over tests or standardized measures of mastery because it does not deal with bits and scraps singly in a "bead-stringing" fashion, but brings together a number of products that demonstrate mastery of a variety of interrelated skills and/or concepts.

Such a portfolio, like a window, looks two ways: in at past performance and out to future performance. It can serve as a basis for planning for the future by demonstrating past mastery, and by so demonstrating, also serve as a credential. This type of portfolio is of more interest to outsiders — next year's teachers, program evaluators, college admissions and placement persons, and so on. To the extent that such a portfolio is handled in a celebratory rather than a judgmental manner, it can also enhance student commitment to learning.

For the past five years in my senior Advanced Placement and college preparatory classes, I have asked students to assemble a portfolio that shows mastery of skills learned through the year.

This includes writing a synopsis, précis, paraphrase, summary, footnotes, and bibliography, as well as best examples of several composing techniques and modes of discourse and samples of both library research and original action research. This portfolio shows far more than the single-focus three-hour AP exam can ever show, and for students who do not take AP exams or seek advanced placement, it can enable their college instructors to know them better.

A student recently returned to tell me that her freshman English professor had opened the semester by asking, "Does anyone have anything from your high school work that you would like me to see?" That is a wonderful question and every freshman instructor should ask it. After reading the student's senior year portfolio, her professor exempted several assignments and gave the student more advanced work. That was exactly what I had in mind when I assigned the portfolio.

Credential portfolios such as these are gradually winning consideration in college admissions and placement decisions. Certainly, students entering college should go forward from where they are rather than spend the freshman year doing things they already know how to do. A wide range of learning experiences in high school should provide a wide range of credentials, and should be provided for their own merits rather than for college expectations.

But most important of all, if we want to encourage and celebrate real learning, then a portfolio is indispensable ...

A "What I Have Done" portfolio, something like those books we did a decade ago, intended to be a showcase of achievement and talent, includes the best work of any kind produced in that course. This is something to rejoice in, to treasure, and something perhaps some day to be discovered in the attic and enjoyed by grandchildren.

All four of these types of portfolios appear in my classroom. They are not exclusive of one another; all are likely to emerge from the daily learning experiences in which we are engaged.

My personal portfolio program has grown organically as I changed my ideas about learning and my methods of instruction over the years. As I change them further, no doubt other types of portfolios will emerge. Right now, I am thinking of a photographer's portfolio that I saw which was selected around the theme of "Seasons." How could we construct a themed portfolio in my classes? What themes would my students choose? How would they select works to illustrate their themes? What would I, and they, see in the collections? The possibilities intrigue me, and I want to present the idea to the students later on.

At present, I am the only teacher in my rural school who is working with portfolios. Neither our local system nor the state of North Carolina has prescribed portfolios. I am free to explore their possibilities, fortunate in not having had external expectations or dictations to restrict my growth. I try to help my students to be equally fortunate. Sometimes I think we in education today are so tied to assessment that we forget that our students will live a long time after they leave us, and that their continuing intellectual and emotional growth is the only assessment that truly counts.

The Teacher's Role in Portfolio Assessment

Joni Chancer

A California teacher finds the role of teachers crucial to the success of student-owned portfolios. She highlights specific classroom practices that prepare students to select and reflect successfully on their writing and reading.

"If portfolios are about self-selection of representative pieces of writing and reflection that only the student can do, then doesn't it follow that the teacher's role in this type of assessment should be minimal?"

As a teacher consultant of the California Writing Project, I am frequently asked this question by teachers who are interested in changing the way they assess their students. As a classroom teacher committed to student-owned portfolio assessment, I was challenged by this same question when I first began using portfolios with my students.

I first heard about portfolios at a conference on assessment held in Los Angeles four years ago. It was called "Beyond the Bubble," and brought the issues of assessment out of the closet and into the center of educational research and discussion. I particularly recall one session in which Dennie Palmer Wolf described the portfolios developed by students of art, music, and writing classes as part of a university-based research project. I was especially struck by her closing statement, which I scribbled into my notebook and underlined three times: "The portfolio is more than a collection of work; it is a conscious statement of growth." That statement must be made by the student, but it is a statement that can be supported and enhanced by an ongoing writing and reading program in which the teacher has an active, essential role as designer, facilitator, coach, and researcher. I don't just stand on the sidelines. I teach.

Using portfolios with my students has changed the way I teach. I have learned to become an observer, to take notes and reflect, to view my teaching as my own personal portfolio to revise and refine. I have discovered that although reflection and the selection of the contents of the portfolio certainly belong to my students, reflection can be taught. It works proportionally: the more ownership I give to my students in self-assessment, the more critical my role becomes. It is the teacher who sets in place the conditions and the structures for what will eventually become a portfolio culture.

In this article I will share the classroom practices I have experimented with and refined in my personal continuing re-search project. The students I describe are fourth, fifth, and sixth grade students from two schools: Oak Hills Elementary School in Agoura, California, and Las Colinas School in Camarillo, Califor-nia. Both schools are in suburban residential areas about forty-five miles northwest of Los Angeles. While there is no single dominant second language group, nearly one-fifth of my students at Oak Hills Elementary are from Middle Eastern, Asian, or Pacific Island countries. Our parent community cares very much about grades, achievement, and the high expectations required for eventual admittance to a university. The spirit of portfolios required some-thing of a shift in attitudes about learning and growth. This was growth that could not be captured in a single grade or a single score. The final collection, selections, and reflections of the stu-dents, as evidenced by the portfolios, convinced the parents of the value of this type of assessment more than any of my words. What blossomed by the end of the year began in September as carefully planted and gradually nurtured seeds.

Starting With Mini-Lessons: Purposeful Play

A purpose of portfolios is to allow students an opportunity or a context for reflection and self-assessment. As part of the reflective process, they frequently consider such questions as:

Why did I write this piece?

Where did I get my ideas?

Who is the audience, and how did that affect the piece?

Was this piece (or parts of it) easy to write? Why?

Was this piece (or parts of it) difficult to write? Why?

What parts flowed and what parts took more time?

What parts did I rework? What were my revisions?

If I received response, what was it? What did others like about my piece? What suggestions did they make?

What am I most satisfied with in this piece, and/or not satisfied with in this piece?

What are skills I worked on in this piece?

Did I try something new?

What elements of writer's craft enhanced my story?

What might I change? How does this compare to other pieces I have written?

Do I have a 'style' that typically characterizes my writing, and does this piece reflect that style?

Did something I read influence my writing?

Is this piece representative of a particular genre or type of writing? What attributes of the genre are reflected in this piece?

What did I learn, or what will the reader learn?

What do I want the reader to know about this piece?

Where will I go from here? Will I publish it? Share it? Expand it? Toss it? File it?

I can't imagine a student answering all these questions about any one piece, nor are these questions meant to constitute a reflection checklist. However, these questions do seem to be addressed frequently by my students when they tell the story of a particular piece.

For example, Maria (a sixth grade student) included a story in her portfolio entitled "No Final Good-bye."

No Final Good-bye

My mother's illness began during an undiagnosed case of rheumatic faver. Her family didn't recognize the signs of the fever because her brother had just died in a boating accident. They thought she was just faking her illness to get some attention.

The lack of treatment for the fever resulted in serious damage to the heart. The doctor's prediction for a normal life was grim. They told her that she would not live past 20 and certainly not have any children.

But she defied their predictions and became a successful business woman, married, had my older brother and me and was a great housewife.

Gradually, after all these years, her heart began to fail.

I really wasn't aware of how serious her condition was, but I knew there was something wrong with my mother that no one was telling me or wanted me to know. I didn't want to go any place with my friends or go to school because I thought she would be gone when I got home. I cried at night knowing she wouldn't be alive and well much longer.

At this time it was near Thanksgiving and everyone in my family was in sort of a fake happiness. Sort of like a false front on an old store; something to cover up the real thing.

Right before Thanksgiving my mother flew back East to a famous heart clinic. The doctors told her of an experimental operation to have new valves put in her heart. But she came back depressed and her hopes for a normal life shattered after the doctors at the clinic told her that she was too old for the operation. She was forty-three and the cut-off age was thirty-nine.

For me the time while she was away was torture. I kept telling myself that my mother would come back and not have to worry about her heart ever again. But then a little voice inside my head told me to face the facts and deal with whatever came up.

Thanksgiving Day my mother went to the hospital and came back, only to have more medicine to take. The doctors could do nothing for her. But even though she had the medicine, she grew weaker. My fears were becoming reality.

I tried to deny what was happening because it was easier to just forget about it. I just wanted to believe that she would jump up, and be well again for the rest of her life, just as she had been before. I wanted everything to be back to normal.

Several days before Christmas, I woke up in the middle of the night to the concerned voice of my father calling the doctor. A few minutes later I was downstairs watching the ambulance attendants place my mother on a stretcher. I stood there watching the tail lights of the ambulance fade into the darkened road. I never saw my mother alive again.

The next morning my father woke me and told me that my mother had died at the hospital, in her sleep, without pain.

'No!' I screamed. 'She can't be dead! They probably got the wrong people mixed up!'

'She's dead,' my father said and walked out of the room.

The funeral was the next day. I dreaded the thought of seeing the casket being lowered into the ground.

When my family got to the funeral home, I went right over to the casket and looked in. There my mother lay in her best silk dress, with her face and hands chalk white. I reached to pick up her hand, but I dropped it, feeling it was ice cold.

This was truly our final good-bye.—Maria (sixth grade)

In her letter introducing her portfolio, Maria shares the following story and reflection about the piece with her readers:

> *'No Final Good-bye' is a true story, and I surprised my writing group with it. It is the story of a girl whose mother dies from heart disease. It is written in the first person, so some of the kids thought it was about me. Well, my mother is still alive! But they thought the story was really sad and some of them even started to cry when they read it. When I was done reading the story to them they didn't want to respond. They said they were too sad, but I wanted them to tell me what they thought I had done a good job of in the story. I told them that the story is really written about my grandmother, told from my mother's point of view. I interviewed my mom, and then told the story as if she were writing it when she was my age. The next day they gave me response. Everyone liked the metaphors and similes in my story and how I used them to show my feelings. Mrs. Chancer liked the transitions and the pacing. I liked how I used the point of view of my mother and convinced my writing group this was real.*

It is clear that Maria is a writer refining her craft. She knows how similes and metaphors can make her writing more interesting. She knows the emotional power of writing and how to sequence and pace the retelling of events to capture a reader's empathy. She makes conscious choices about point of view and recognizes the effect of writing with voice. And yet in the beginning of the year, her reflections focused on her "neat cursive" and "excellent spelling," and the length of her stories. What made the difference? I observed that Maria's reflections became richer, more meaningful and specific as she was gradually introduced to elements of the writer's craft.

Throughout the year a focus of our writing workshop is to play with these various craft techniques, and mini-lessons have allowed the play to become purposeful. The design and teaching of the mini-lessons are the aspect of my writing and reading program in which I feel the most creative and effective. Working with students during craft mini-lessons is like guiding artists in a studio. The chapters devoted to mini-lessons in books by Donald Graves, Lucy Calkins, Nancie Atwell, and Rebekah Caplan make a significant difference in my own writing and the writing of my students. I recommend the books of these authors to any teachers interested in designing or refining a classroom writing workshop.

Typically, a mini-lesson in my class begins with the sharing of literature: excerpts from favorite books, lines of poems, favorite dialogue, interesting character descriptions, even provocative titles and first lines of novels. For example, one such mini-lesson on dialogue might begin with a quick Reader's Theater from Judy Blume's *Tales of a Fourth Grade Nothing*, a book filled with humorous, engaging conversation. After the reading, we talk about what Judy Blume did that captured us as readers. The children respond with comments such as these:

> *She writes like kids really talk.*
>
> *She doesn't use the word said over and over. She uses different words for said.*
>
> *Sometimes the sentences are really short or not even complete, and another character breaks in with a line.*
>
> *She tells you what the characters are doing while they are talking so you can imagine it in your mind.*
>
> *Sometimes she tells you what the characters say and what they are thinking.*

Before the mini-lesson begins, I think about dialogue myself and jot down a few notes. If the children have trouble getting started in their observations, I ask them to look at a particular line, passage, or even a word. I don't tell them what to think, I just focus their attention. As they make their observations, I record them on an overhead. Donald Graves (1991) suggests saving the overheads for future reference. I have found this to be an invaluable suggestion, and frequently find myself saying things like, "Remember when we talked about dialogue and you said sometimes the author lets you know what a character says and then what the character thinks? Let's look at what you discovered about dialogue again." The overhead goes up. "Now I'll read a passage from Christopher's story. Tell me if you hear places where his dialogue is really working. The things we recorded on the overhead might help you."

Along with the overhead, the children and I save excerpts from their pieces or nominate entire pieces of writing that are good demonstrations of writer's craft. I use these excerpts over and over in subsequent years. The children look through our Writer's Craft binder with pride, and see examples of their writing alongside passages from published authors of the literature we read together and individually.

Mini-lessons engage children in listening, focusing attention, learning about writing through connections with reading, experimenting, sharing and refining. These are the attitudes and activities that eventually foster reflection in the portfolio.

Teaching Reflection:
Translating to "Student-Speak"

With the recent emphasis on authentic assessments, we as teachers have been introduced to a new vocabulary. Grade books are no longer at the heart of evaluation. We converse with each other about a child's developing fluency, confidence, and experience as reader and a writer; we understand what these terms imply. They represent very important considerations in the evaluation of our students. The conversation, however, should not be limited to teachers. Ideally, I want my students to be able to reflect upon their self-perceived growth. Beginning in the first week of school, the children and I begin considering these elements of fluency, confidence, and experience, translated into "student-speak." The focus is never negative, but encourages honest recognition of strengths, areas to work on, and subsequent goal-setting.

Fluency is a topic in our initial discussions and mini-lessons. Many children believe they should read and write effortlessly if they are "really good at it." They are often surprised and relieved to acknowledge that while they may be fluent readers of particular types of books, certain books (textbooks, information books or even poetry) may require more attention and slower-paced concentration; maybe even two or three readings. As an example, I share with my students how I must read computer software instruction manuals slowly, sometime even orally, before the message clicks and I truly comprehend the information. Sometimes I need to read the first paragraph or page of a book a few times before I connect with the story and subsequently go on to read with more speed and fluency. I often choose to read poems two or three times, and somehow the meaning becomes clearer with each reading. Before long the children begin to share examples of instances when they read and write effortlessly, and other times when they need to slow down and "work a little harder."

This is a significant breakthrough for many of my students. Never before have they considered their own personal patterns of literacy. The discussions open the door not just to reflection, but also to strategies for learning and personal goal-setting. Children learn not to be easily discouraged. This does not mean that they are poor readers. That acknowledgement and acceptance opens the door for some children to what Frank Smith (1988) calls "the club of literacy." Until that door is opened, these students may stay outside the circle of the literate community and resist any consideration of goal-setting or reflection of strengths and areas to work on, as this sample demonstrates:

> Brian (sixth grade): *I guess I read kind of slowly, at least slower than a lot of other kids. I read a few pages and then I stop and think about what I read, and what the setting is, and I try to get into the book. It works for me and it's just the way I read.*

For other readers, their awareness of fluency patterns indicates their growing maturity and development. We talk about how more experienced and reflective readers sense and acknowledge the different ways they read:

Amanda (fifth grade): *When I read* The Doll Hospital *I read it quickly. The vocabulary wasn't difficult and the print wasn't small. The plot was easy to understand. But sometimes I reread a book when the author changes settings quickly, or if the book has harder vocabulary, like in* Harriet the Spy. *Then I take a little longer.*

Jessica (fifth grade): *I sometimes have to read a page over when a book starts off with a lot of characters, like in* Anne of Green Gables *or* The Witch of Blackbird Pond. *Another time when I sometimes slow down my reading or reread parts is when the author uses words I don't understand, like the old-fashioned words in* Little Women.

Brendan (fifth grade): *The books I breeze through are the funny and humorous books, for example Roald Dahl and Judy Blume books. Especially* Matilda! *They have lots of dialogue and I think that makes them easy and fun to read.*

Fluency in writing is also a topic for discussion from the very first day. For example, as we spend time together in writing workshop, I invite my students to consider if they are writing longer stories. Perhaps it is easier for them to write in a particular genre or style. Are they noticing that they are writing faster? Is it easier to get the words down on their paper? Do they know what to say and how to get started?

Our conversation generally brings us to a consideration of strategies they may want to try. Some find it helpful to talk about a story before they begin to write. Other students cluster their ideas in webs on their paper. Some of my students find it easier to compose on the computer, others seek a quiet place and a familiar notebook or journal.

We talk about spelling, writing in cursive vs. manuscript, and what to do when either of these considerations becomes a roadblock. We discuss why fluency is important to writing and how personal expectations for first draft perfection can get in the way.

Eventually, the discussions come around to the value and freedom that revision brings to the process of writing. Knowing that they can add things to their stories after receiving response or rereading a piece, reorganizing their thoughts on paper, scratching out words or whole sections, explaining things more or polishing up certain descriptions give students faith that they can jot down ideas for fluency first, and refinement and form can follow.

Eventually, fluency becomes an important focus in portfolio reflections. In their introductory letters to their portfolios, students frequently comment on their fluency as both writers and readers, as these two examples show:

I think I'm a very good writer. When I write I sit down the ideas just come to me! It's easy for me to write. When I write you will see I write with detail and description. You can picture it in your mind! My writing is humorous and adventurous. When I write it takes me into another world. I have written all kinds of stories. Mysteries, reports, fanticy, letters, eassys (essays), personal times, anything! No matter if it's an eassy or biografy I include humor, or something to make it interesting and sound like me! I like writing true stories the most because they are easyer to write about. I think I'm a much better writer this year than I was last year and I think the Cree Indian Naming Poem I wrote tells a lot about me.

Writes Like the Wind

Her name tells of how it was with her.
It was then, September of 1991,
that she knew,
she must be a writer.
Her pencil just moved across the paper, magically.
She wrote with creativity and humor.
The words flowed like wind out of her head
and onto the paper.

When she was done,
she was satisfied with her work.
She had **Written Like the Wind.**
—Lauren Roth

I am a good writer and I am fluent once I have an idea.
Sometimes it is hard for me to think of what I will write
about. The genre studies we did in writing and reading
helped me learn new ways to write this year. It was easier to
plan my stories and then my ideas flowed better. My favorite
stories that I wrote were: Blue Boy Is Missing, a mystery
story; Stephanie and the Magical Book, a fantasy; and The
Curse of the Swan, a fairy tale. I like writing fairy tales,
fantasy stories and mysteries the most. I have improved as a
writer by becoming more descriptive. A goal I have for next
year is to write a good adventure story.
—Elizabeth

Both students clearly recognize how considerations of fluency affect their processes as writers and readers.

Using Conversation: Reflection in Reading

In December of the first year that I used portfolios with my students, I asked them to "reflect on their personal growth in reading." Not surprisingly, many children responded with uncertainty and puzzled expressions. I quickly figured out that the question was too general and abstract and needed to be broken down to considerations the children would find more meaningful. I also recognized we needed a context or setting for ongoing conversations about books and reading. I didn't want the reflections to be the point of the discussions, but a natural part of an ongoing process.

I stumbled into what has become a favorite part of our portfolio classroom — book clubs. I told a teacher friend that I wanted to capture the elements of my adult book club: the sharing, excitement, and anticipation of discovering really good books. I know how powerfully influenced I am by someone else's enthusiastic endorsement of a particular book or author. Nancie Atwell, in her book *In the Middle* (1987), beautifully describes a structure for sharing self-selected books: reading workshop. My book clubs are a slightly modified spin-off of Atwell's model.

With my fourth and fifth grade students, an equal emphasis is placed upon the oral conversations about books after sharing Lit Letters in an established group. I meet with my students every week in small book clubs of five to seven heterogeneously grouped students. Each club member comes to the meeting with a Lit Letter about a self-selected book. In their letters I encourage the children to consider questions such as:

- *What is the title/author/genre/setting/number of pages?*
- *Why did you choose this book?*
- *Briefly, what is the book about?*
- *Who are the characters? What are they like? Do they change?*
- *Why might someone else want to read this book?*
- *Did this book remind you of other books you have read?*
- *What is your overall feeling about this book?*
- *Did you learn anything from this book? What?*
- *What is your favorite part?*
- *What will you remember the most about this book?*
- *Do you have favorite lines or quotes from the book?*
- *Was this book easy? Difficult? Challenging? Just about right? Why?*

The questions focus not just on "comprehension," but also on more affective, personal considerations that reflect their processes as readers. Few children answer all the questions, and some children do not choose to address them at all. Often, however, the letters seem to be loosely structured around these considerations, as this letter demonstrates:

Dear club Members,

I just finished a book called Streams To the River, River to the Sea. *Its author is Scott O'Dell. Its genre is Historical fiction. Its through the Lewis and Clark expedition and has 163 pages.*

I chose this book because everybody in my book club read it and said it had wild adventure and true love.

Briefly the book is about a Shoshone girl who got captured by attack. The Minnetarees who captured her betted on her to marry a cruel trader who came often to trade. Charbonneau was his name. Sacagawea was her real name and she had to marry the man without even knowing him. She and her husband join with Lewis and Clark. They needed Sacagawea to show them the way through her hometown which was jagged and hard to climb.

The characters are Sacagawea who is a brave Indian girl with lots of troubles. Captain Lewis, a rugged man with his brain as a compass and Captain Clark a strong man who knows whats best for his crew and others.

No they do not change.

My overall feeling for the book is high thanks to the description in the book and the quality of adventure.

I will remember when Sacagawea got captured it was so sad.

This book was challenging to read because of the strange names like Charbonneau.

> *Sincerely,*
>
> *Young (grade four)*

Children clearly address their letters to each other, not to the teacher. The other club members then jump off from the letter to a lively conversation. Frequently students jot down the titles of books that interest them, and I often ask the children to come prepared with a favorite excerpt to read aloud.

Motivation, comprehension, and attention to the process of reading are evident in every letter and group conversation. One of our most memorable discussions focused on a statement one club member made that "Gary Paulson's book *Hatchet* is a boy's book." What followed was a very animated conversation that bordered on debate concerning the question of whether a particular book could be genderized. I smiled, remembering how my adult book club argued about the exact same issue.

The book club meeting becomes the context for authentic assessments, providing me with rich opportunities for observation and informal note taking. Frequently during these meetings I ask questions in student-speak that break down the more abstract query of "How have you grown or developed as a reader?" When responding to these questions, the children discuss with each other :

- *If they are reading longer books, 'chapter' books, or if they are reading for longer time periods.*
- *If they are willing to give new books a chance (beyond three pages) before abandoning them.*
- *If they are reading more books.*
- *How they distinguish a 'really good book' from an 'OK' book.*
- *If they appreciate the way an author writes.*
- *If they have favorite authors, or favorite genres.*

Children understand these questions, and their spiral notebooks soon become filled with Lit Letters that clearly demonstrate their development as experienced readers. The weekly conversations inherently guide them toward the metacognition and reflection that is at the heart of the portfolio.

For years children received a single grade in reading comprehension. The teacher, with tests and scores for substantiation, passed sole judgment on how well the students understood what they read. In our portfolio classroom I don't give children fill-in-the-blank comprehension tests, and I look beyond single scores on standardized tests. Through their Lit Letters, conversations, shared oral reading experiences, book projects and journal entries, it becomes obvious to me, and more importantly to the students, that they understand what they read.

I am not surprised when most of my students include their spirals filled with their book club Lit Letters in their final show-case portfolios.

Reflecting on Writing:
Not a Twice-a-Year Endeavor

By the middle of the year my students' writing folders are bursting with writing. These pieces were written with red hot intensity weeks or months earlier. That intensity is sometimes forgotten when piece follows piece and students move on to new projects. I often wished I could capture the essence of our confer-ences about particular stories and the students' verbal and in-sightful oral comments about the history of each piece: why they chose to write a story; what were challenging parts to write; what techniques of writer's craft they experimented with; what revi-sions they made; and what response they received. Because I know the importance these considerations and reflections play in the portfolio process, I now encourage the children to record their responses during our final conference about stories they have revised and plan to publish.

I demonstrate this process with an example of my own writing. After an oral sharing of something I've written I share the history of the piece. Working with my students , I have created a "Thinking About My Story" reflection sheet that helps record details and thoughts that might otherwise be forgotten.

Some students complete the sheet independently before the final conference about the piece; others seem to reflect best orally, almost conversationally. They point out particular words, sen-tences or passages they like, "tough parts to write," new tech-niques they experimented with, and revisions they made. As they talk and point, I jot down some of their reflections. Whether the sheet is completed independently or in collaboration with the teacher, it is stapled or clipped to the drafts and published versions of the piece and saved in the cumulative folder. When students read their final drafts aloud, the sharing of their "Thinking About My Story" sheet is often included in a whole class conference and student-led demonstration of the reflection process. As the children look through their folders to choose their showcase portfolio selections the "Thinking About My Story" notes take them right back to the conference and the moments of discovery and reflection. From demonstration to conversation to sharing, reflection becomes a regular practice.

Integrating Selection and Reflection: The Introductory Letter to the Portfolio

The first year I used portfolios with my students, I was especially cautious when the time came for the selection of pieces and the composing of the letters introducing the portfolios. I knew there was a fine line between encouraging students to consider various aspects of what a portfolio might be and prescribing what the portfolios should be. I was especially concerned about those children who appear to be naturally task-oriented and, despite all of my cautions, often almost unconsciously infer: "This is what she seems to want so that is what I will do."

It made sense to start by discussing various professionals who use portfolios in real-life situations. We talked about architects, advertising consultants, artists, and even fashion models. The children caught on right away to the idea that an architect who has designed a wide range of buildings including stores, office buildings, schools, museums, and homes would be foolish to include in his portfolio only photographs and plans of twelve banks he has designed if he hoped to win a contract to design a new, model city. On the other hand, if he hoped to be selected to design a series of new buildings for a major banking corporation, a portfolio featuring banks would be a good idea. Children see that the contents of portfolios can be flexible, depending upon their purposes.

With my fourth and fifth grade students, the purpose of the first portfolio commonly focuses on showing several things: best work; a range of work; revisions and process pieces; first drafts, second drafts, final drafts and published books; and often the pieces the student cared about the most. I want my writers and readers to be impressed with themselves, to say, "Wow! When I show you this body of work, there will be no doubt that I am a writer and a reader!" And so we brainstorm together what kinds of selections they might make in putting together the portfolios.

Frequently, I share my own portfolio with the students and I talk about the reasons behind my selections. I read them my own letter of introduction to the contents I have chosen. Sometimes I show them copies I have made of student portfolios from previous years. I am very careful to share several varied portfolios that clearly demonstrate a range of possibilities. Looking at and hearing aloud the introductory letters written by other students is critical. Students need to hear from other students. It makes a powerful statement about ownership.

The children are eager to review the contents of their folders a second time, with purposeful reflection. As they select the pieces for their portfolios they jot down their reasons for the selections. Finally they are ready to compose their introductory letters.

Student ownership is encouraged, demonstrated, and celebrated by the teacher. The choices are theirs, but the possibilities have been expanded. The children quickly come to see that there is no single "right way" to put together a portfolio. Their letters reflect their voices, their purposes, and their individual statements of growth:

> *Dear Reader,*
>
> *My name is Tamara and I am in sixth grade at Los Nogales School. I enjoy the beach, going shopping, watching TV, reading and writing. I have written MANY stories this year!*
>
> *The first piece you will read is a description of Tahiti. I haven't been to Tahiti so I had to try to imagine it. I looked at travel books and drew a picture of it. This was the first time I really tried to use focused descriptions and sensory descriptions in my writing.*

The next piece is my autobiography. I tried to tell you more than the facts about me. I put in things I like and things I don't like and even the things I hate! I put in some special memories, too. Doing the timeline of my life helped me organize this piece.

The next piece is one of my favorites. I published it into a book. I made up a character called Eek the Squeek. He's a mouse detective. I got the idea from reading a book called Nate the Great. *Mysteries are hard to write. You really have to have the plot make sense! You have to have clues that make sense too. I tried to give Eek a personality. I loved doing the illustrations and the cover of the book, too. I tried to write a book little kids would like.*

The next story is 'Halloween Night.' I like the dialogue and the description of the setting. I had to work on the plot of this story so I wouldn't give the ending away too soon.

It's Locked *is another book I published. In this story we were supposed to figure out a problem and plan the solution and then write a story. I worked hard on describing the characters and building up to the part where I describe the problem. I tried to make the dialogue sound real and the description of the stuff that went on in class. I think this is one of my best two stories.*

'I Can Remember' tells about a shirt I hated wearing. I tried to describe what it looked like, and also why I hated wearing it so much. I think I did a good job as you will see. I HATED that stupid shirt!

'My First Puppy' was hard to write. It is a true story about my puppy. I wanted a dog SO BAD, and when we finally got one, he died after a little while. I tried to tell how much I wanted him and how sad I was when he died.

This year I learned a lot about writing. I learned about focused descriptions, using five sense descriptions, show not tell, specific verbs and not using the same words over and over. When you read my stories you will see that I experi-

mented with different kinds of leads and dialogue. I learned
to put feelings in my stories. That was maybe most impor-
tant. Anyway, I wrote A LOT, but these are the BEST that
I want you to read.
    Sincerely,
    Tamara

Taking My Turn: Portfolios to be Passed On

During the last week of school the final student-selected
showcase portfolios are complete, and they have been shared and
celebrated. Sitting on my desk I have a portfolio and folder of
collected pieces from each of the students in my class. Now it is my
turn to add my voice to the story of each child's growth as a reader
or writer during the time I spent with them. I review their
showcase portfolio which we discussed together during the final
portfolio conference. I also read through the folder containing the
pieces which were not chosen by the student. If the receiving
teacher in the following grade chooses to participate in this
process and has indicated to me what he or she hopes to learn
about the new students coming from my class, I consider which
pieces might be included in a portfolio to be passed on. I typically
make a copy of the student's favorite piece and the letter introducing the portfolio. I look for two or three other pieces that demonstrate the growth, or in some cases, any inconsistent development
I have observed during the year. I look for the pieces that will tell
the story of a child: pieces with voice and personal style. I try to
vary the selections to demonstrate the range of writing. I like to
include at least one piece of totally unassisted writing. Options
vary according to my purposes and, ultimately, the eventual
audience of this portfolio.

Finally, I choose one particular piece and quickly summarize
my impressions of the student as evidenced in the writing. This is
my opportunity to let my voice be heard. At first the summarizing
was difficult and time-consuming, but as I became more experienced I found the words flew from my mind to the computer. I am
now able to complete thirty-four summaries in an afternoon. I
don't need to analyze numbers or correct final tests; I know these

Book cover by Wendy Terada

children so well that their stories literally leap from the pages of their writing. Receiving teachers have commented on how surprisingly accurate even the shortest summaries prove to be. The following examples are written about end-of-the-year fourth grade students. Each summary is attached to a sample which I feel demonstrates the student's strengths at this point of the year:

Marc is a joy and a challenge in many ways. This child is verbally articulate and loves to talk! I am often impressed by the wealth of his general knowledge about a wide range of topics. He listens (rather selectively), but when he is interested he retains information and small details to an amazing degree. However, his fluency and expressiveness totally break down when it comes to written language. Marc avoids writing. One or two sentences are his limit. He is quite satisfied with pieces of this length and is not really motivated to rethink his pieces. He will add detail at a verbal level, so my main strategy when working with him is to take frequent dictation, help him publish on the computer (a real motivation), and encourage him to share his writing orally with the rest of the class.

This piece is probably an example of Eric at his most fluent and expressive. Eric was new to our school this year and came from a school where his mother reports children had limited experience with writing and where emphasis was placed on correctness, not imagination. He started the year hesitant and reluctant to write more than a sentence or two. Even with prewriting experiences, conferences, discussions with other children, etc., he did not seem to break through to fluency. His basic skills are usually good, but his pieces are so short it is at times difficult to evaluate his editing abilities. He hasn't felt ready to take risks with description and dialogue like most of the others in class.

Just this past month Eric has demonstrated more motivation and he has also shown more interest in independent reading. He moved on from the easier Judy Blume books (which he loved and reread) to more challenging books like Indian in the Cupboard *and* On My Honor. *About the same time he started taking off with our genre studies in writing. The discussions and structures helped him get started and gave him a plan. With this fairy tale, he really worked on developing plot. Interestingly, he has become more verbal in class as well. He loves the computer and is now publishing stories at home. Inserting graphics seems to motivate him to expand short pieces. He is now feeling pleased with himself as a writer.*

Portfolios are not just about checklists, record sheets, and file folders. The preparation for portfolio assessment is much more than a two or three day process of review and selection. Preparation begins the first day of school. This type of assessment belongs to the student, yet the teacher has never had a more important, active role in setting in motion the structures that support a portfolio classroom.

When the final day of school is over and I have hugged the last child, locked my cupboards, taken down the pictures, drawings, projects, and poems, I often find myself caught up in my own reflections. Portfolios, I decide, are a lot like parenthood. When children are ready to leave home it is tempting to want to tell them how to live their lives. But instead you bite your tongue and tell yourself you have to trust that the day-by-day life you have lived together, the joy and pain, disappointments and celebrations, that are woven into the fabric of your family have grounded and shaped your children into individuals who are ready to make decisions independently. Likewise, as a teacher I must trust that the ongoing program that began the first day of school has prepared my students to make decisions about the contents, the reflections, and the self-assessment that are the core of the portfolio. The literary community we have created together is characterized by children who are confident and well prepared to share their strengths, goals, and discoveries about who they are as writers, readers, and ultimately, individuals.

References

Anthony, R. J. (1991). *Evaluating literacy.* Portsmouth, NH: Heinemann.

Calkins, L. M. (1991). *Living between the lines.* Portsmouth, NH: Heinemann.

Caplan, R. (1984). *Writers in training.* Palo Alto, CA: Dale Seymour.

Goodman, K. S., Goodman, Y. M., & Hood, W. J. (Eds.). (1989). *The whole language evaluation book.* Portsmouth, NH: Heinemann.

Graves, D. H. (1991). *Build a literate classroom.* Portsmouth, NH: Heinemann.

Parry, J., & Hornsby, D. (1985). *Write on: A conference approach to writing.* Portsmouth, NH: Heinemann.

Reif, L. (1992). *Seeking diversity.* Portsmouth, NH: Heinemann.
Smith, F. (1988). *Joining the literacy club: Further essays into education.* Portsmouth, NH: Heinemann.

Tierney, R. J., Carter, M. A., & Densai, L. E. (1991). *Portfolio assessment in the reading-writing classroom.* Norwood, MA: Christopher-Gordon.

Portfolios as Discovery

Mary Kay Deen

A Mississippi teacher looks at portfolios through the eyes of three primary children. She credits their reflections with providing the missing link in evaluation and in her classroom.

My Story

When I first entered school I was a confident little girl, eager to learn. However, I soon discovered there were many things in school I could not do well. I found that no one cared that I could watch squirrels frolic in treetops and rabbits scamper in berry thickets, sing "Zippity Do Da," and skip down unlevel hillsides all at the same time without falling. These things were not school-smart. No one cared that I knew the touch of moss to bare feet, the beauty of Mama's four-o'clocks in the late afternoon, and the call of a whippoorwill. No one cared that I could tell original stories or that I had made teacakes with my grandmother, dried peaches and apples in summer sunshine, watched fern fronds unfurl and birds build their homes. In school, birds were not celebrated for their songs, their flight, their beauty. They were reading group names — blue birds, red birds, and yellow birds. I was a yellow bird — not a goldfinch, a yellow bird, and yellow birds couldn't read well.

There were other things in school to show me what I could not do — things called tests. There were tests in reading, tests in arithmetic, tests in spelling and big tests that came in a book, a whole book!

My testing nightmare intensified in May, 1960, when I was told that I was not college material because my test scores were too low. I was embarrassed and frightened that my friends and family might learn about this awful secret. I was afraid of going to college, but more terrified of not going, and so I went, terrified of tests and terrified of failure.

I graduated from college, taught school and even entered a graduate program, conditionally, of course, due to my low test scores. Rather than advance through the maze of academia, I have involved myself in independent study, conference participation, and classroom research as vehicles for professional growth.

For me school was no safe harbor until the summer of 1991, when I met some teachers in the South Mississippi Writing/ Thinking Institute who discovered, under those layers of test "cannots," my fern fronds, teacakes, birds, and stories.

During the fall of 1991, I was invited to participate in a Portfolio Assessment Task Force sponsored by the Mississippi Writing/ Thinking Project. This was just what I was looking for, an alternative to testing. I quickly learned that portfolio development and assessment fostered respect for students and placed responsibility on students, thus empowering them to learn.

This was the kind of learning and assessment that encouraged risk-taking, where experts are born in the midst of their own discoveries.

The Children's Stories

At North Bay Elementary School in Bay St. Louis, Mississippi, where beaches meet the Gulf of Mexico, students in this kindergarten through third grade school reflect the people and life in our small town. Some families here survive, put meals on their tables, by harvesting seafood; others enjoy the water for sport fishing and boating; and many delight in the pure aesthetic pleasure of the Gulf. Our school of 300 students takes all children: privileged ones, ones with little opportunity, and "Main Street America" children.

I introduced portfolios to my second grade students as a collection of items selected for a particular purpose, and together we prepared a plan for developing our writing portfolios. Our plan

The Aboriginals Art

This is a goanna. Goannas live in Australia. Long-ago goannas were painted on rocks by pepol called aborigines. The aborigines thought if they painted an animal on a rock that when it died it's sprit would come back. To make that happen they painted bouth the inside and the outside of the animal.

The aborigines used disigns in the animals that they painted. Some of the other animals they painted kangaroos, long-neck turtles, thunderman, burramundi, and echidnas.

By Ashley Ready

Goanna — Australian lizard

included purposes and what needed to be in the portfolio in order to meet those purposes. We also talked about when and how the portfolio selections would be made and who would make them.

We agreed on three purposes for developing the portfolios: to help the students see their growth and development as writers over a period of time; to help the students develop self-confidence by celebrating their accomplishments as writers; and to help the teacher see the students' growth as writers.

We easily recognized that to see growth over time we would need writing samples that reflected a wide span of time. In order to see both growth and development we had to keep "clues," evidence of how our writing and thinking had developed. The writing process was our guide. We decided to keep all of our work on each piece in our portfolio — our brainstorming, "sloppy copy," revision, final copy, and reflection (our writing about our writing and ourselves) — for they were our evidence.

Our first struggle with change came when we began talking about the selection process. I realized how little power my children assumed they had, for they did not even consider that they could make their portfolio selections. However, with more discussion about writers and the choices and decisions they make in the process of writing, the children realized that writers know their own work better than anyone else. Writers know which piece is their best, their most important, and their favorite. Since the children were the writers who were developing portfolios, of course they should select the pieces! As a security net, I asked their permission to make a selection. They granted my request, and they also gave their parents an opportunity to choose a piece for their portfolio.

Each month the children perused their writing folders for possible portfolio pieces. Usually they knew precisely which piece they wanted to select. Occasionally, however, they asked their peers or me for help with the selection. We would listen to each other read and offer each other encouragement; but the choice, the actual selection, was always made by the writer.

Meghan

I felt happy for reading my work. first it's like a moon then sunshine. Sunsine is for reading my work.

This poetic celebration was Meghan's response to her own portfolio. Her growth as a writer and her self-confidence are a reflection of her writing transformation from moon to sunshine.

I kind of like my story. The Fish it has good illustraysons. But there are words speld in cract. So I haft to spele them write. Some words. But wene I grow up I will be a teacher. I will give my class poflyos and they will have a note in their poflyo and I will be proud for myself. For doing hard work. I can fee writing in my hart now that I am a teacher. I like to write and I like to add to my portfolio because it is fun. Wene I write or add on my portflos I get very qwick idas. And I maded a story that I got idas from that portflio. And I dream that I am the best writer in the hole wide world. I now what to do wene I am bord just look at my portfolios.

I observed Meghan's development as a writer in her improvement in fluency, form, and organization, in her excitement when sharing her work, and her extended, focused writing time. These are important, but they pale by comparison to her own assessment. Without her input I would have presented only a sterile teacher observation that in no way reflected the growth she expressed in the "moon" to "sunshine" image. I also would not have captured the hope she shared in her dream or the pleasure she derived from reading her portfolio. Meghan's reflection brought depth and wholeness to the assessment process.

Christa

Christa was a little girl repeating second grade, who prior to this experience had not found her way in school. Her grandmother told me that developing her writing portfolio was the first school pleasure Christa had ever enjoyed.

I was delighted to hear of her happiness, for I remembered well the first time I asked her class to write. Christa found getting started difficult, because I would not tell her what or how much to write. She could only use words she could spell, and she numbered and listed her sentences. They were "correctness sentences" such as "I like my teacher," very neatly penned, for to her that was writing. Christa's end-of-year portfolio reflection revealed that even after a year of writing she still valued her work because of good penmanship.

Christa appeared most comfortable when reflecting on books she had heard or read and when writing about authors she had met through books and interview tapes. Rarely did she find the courage to write her own story without the security of a book or author.

Christa enjoyed writing. She quickly gave me permission to share her portfolio with teachers in other schools. She was thrilled when I returned it with encouraging notes from readers.

In her portfolio reflection, Christa confirmed my observations:

I feel happy about developing my writing this whole year. And I also saw in my portfolio notes that other readers wrote to me. And in the Beginning of the year I felt like I did not want to writ but I love to write now. Yes I would like to writ a nother portfolio folder because I love to write and illactrate and I love to read my writing that I done in the Begining of the year. I can write better because my writing gives you a clear picture of my writing and I can illastrat too. I can read better because I read every day. My portfolio shows me as a writer because use to I write rilly sloppy but now I write nice and that's how my portfolio shows my writing.

Christa's reflection and my observations revealed a child who had been victimized by a skill-based, product-correctness education. This is not an indictment of her teachers, but of an educational philosophy that has often stifled learning and damaged the self-esteem of children.

I was both happy and sad as I read Christa's reflection. I was happy that she liked writing, but disappointed that she still valued her writing as penmanship. I had hoped we had broken that barrier to self-discovery. My disappointment however, was just that — mine, not Christa's, for she felt happy, liked her writing and wanted to make another portfolio.

Christa caught the writer's spirit. When I asked the children if they would like to publish an anthology, she was the first one to begin searching her work for pieces to submit. Christa read and reread her writing, eliminating pieces until she had the ones she wanted to publish. She then took these to her peers for their approval before submitting them to our class book. With their support, she proudly contributed her writing.

Sky

In October, Sky wrote, "I like Mrs. Deen, I like Ms Makdogl I like Ms. Born." He selected this for his portfolio because "i like my teacher."

During February, while studying China, our class read many legends. The following story, "How The White Man Turned Black," was the result of Sky's interest in Chinese legends.

One sun day a boy named Niky was Jumping in the stret in frunt of my Hom. He fell in the mud. Then he got up. Wen he sow he was black he yeled yos! becos he cod not be seen and he cod skar pepel. And his mom saw him came an and she said take a bath you are filithy. And Neky toke a bath. He was mad that the mud came off. He was mud that the mud came off becos he kod be seen then.

Sky also selected this piece for his portfolio. He used a suggested guide and wrote the following reflections on his story, "How The White Man Turned Black."

I selected this piece because *It is my best riteing and I like it becos of the illustrations.*

The best sentence in this piece is *He fell in the mud.* I think it is the best sentence because *i lafe at the sentence becos it is funny.*

55

I revised my sloppy copy. Why? *No I like it this way.*

I got my ideas for this piece from *I got my idea from a lagond caled the magjik wings.* My illustrations help to show my story. *Yes* Why? *becos the illustrations sow the thans i rite.*

What did you enjoy most about the writing process? Why? *Geting to rite a book that make sens.*

What is the piece about? *My piece is about a boy named Niky.*

Do you think your piece is the best piece you can write? Explain your answer. *Yes becos I rot it and I like it.*

Do you think you are a better writer now than you were in September? Why? *yes becos I have more ideas.*

The two pieces and reflections are evidence of Sky's growth as a writer and thinker from October to February. He definitely found his voice, which in turn gave his writing fluency. He wrote with humor, and his story form showed a beginning, a middle, and an end. Sky identified the source of his ideas and he used illustration to support his writing. My notes revealed that Sky wrote fewer pieces than most of his classmates, but there was pleasure for him in the work he produced, and he often spent an entire writing time just staring into space thinking. He could not be hurried.

I know this well, for more often than I like to admit I tried to rush his pondering, his time, the very thing I must also have. Do I view this thing called time as an obstacle to productivity instead of a gift of process?

Sky was a complex little boy who had a strong sense of fairness. When I made mistakes he helped me correct them. For instance, there was the day I decided to let him talk through a reflection before writing it. I thought this might shorten his pre-writing time and get him to "produce" faster. My intentions were to help him not be the last one to finish. Sky became so uneasy that he retreated to October's canned phases. When I told him I could see that this was a mistaken idea of mine and asked him what we should do, he told me he just needed time to think.

Sky struggled to teach me. With gentle persistence he painted rainbows and penned his story. I finally saw that, just as a butterfly's wings need time to dry, Sky needed time to think.

Amy

Amy's end-of the-year portfolio reflection is a detailed self-assessment:

> *I feel happy about developing my writing portfolio this year. I know that if i ceep pragresing like this that I will be a wounderful writer some day. I would love to make another protfolio wile I am on summer brake. The part I liked best is when I was making the story called Rich. I just had a morvalis time making it. It was about to peple named Amy and Zak. One day they went to the caloseum and saw an alligator and it was the persons who oned the caloseum. they cep on coming and eat mash potatoes and gravey. For desert they had pinapple crum cake.*
>
> *What I can do now that I could not do befor is use my talking voice very well. Plus I could not organize or use much detail. But I can do that now.*
>
> *Some things I can do very wel are making the beginning, middle, and ending of my story. Some things I can all so do revision very well.*
>
> *It shows that I like to make poems. It allso shows that I like to write made up storys. What I am strong at doing is using my talking voice, my revision, and sharing. What I can do in my next writing piece to grow as a writer is think about my audiance and most of all my editing. I believe that I want to emprovr my detail and organizing.*

My notes pointed out Amy's acceptance of herself, her appreciation of her own work, her strong writer's voice, her ability to extend story writing over several days, and her eagerness to participate in the revision process. Amy wrote fluently, and she used details to make pictures in the minds of her readers. She often designed pre-writing plans that helped her organize her work.

Amy enjoyed the "sloppy copy" draft for it was a place where, "I can jot down everything that flashes throw my head."

She used pre-writing, drafting, reading, sharing, and revising to make her writing better. She constantly identified ways to improve. Amy was always open to suggestions from others. She was a leader in response group, kind and patient, supportive of the reader, and she helped other children discover their potential. In her portfolio reflection, Amy demonstrated her ability to summarize her growth as a writer.

My observation of Amy was thorough. It was her self-examination, however, and her ability to share her discoveries that completed the image — a little girl who knew the joy of learning, created her own happiness, and found affirmation from within.

Reflections

In each of these children's portfolio stories, it is their reflections on those pieces and themselves that reveal the part that is missing when only the teacher assesses. That missing piece, I believe, is the most important aspect of assessment: the children's perception of their own growth. In portfolio assessment students focus on their own effort, their own process, their own achievement, not their achievement as it is compared to that of someone else. I believe there is empowerment and motivation in discovering one's own progress, empowerment and motivation that energizes the spirit and enhances self-confidence.

As I reviewed our portfolio experience, I came to several conclusions. In a community built around process, portfolio development, and portfolio assessment, these young children and I were empowered to believe in ourselves and others, to accept ourselves and others, and to celebrate our uniquenesses. This kind of empowerment can be seen in Kate's end-of-the-year reflection:

> *I feel very happy about my portfolio because I am getting much better as a writer. I am very happy that my writing is MINE and know body can EVER take it because its mine and I like it VERY much!!!*

Portfolios in which students own the selection process and reflect on their own effort, process, progress, product, and future writing are incredibly valuable in connecting student motivation, instruction, and assessment. Portfolios in which students receive positive written responses from teachers, peers, family, and others help the students build on their strengths, develop self-confidence, increase their understanding of audience, and set goals for their future writing. Student ownership, student reflection, and positive written responses to the student are the elements that dramatically differentiate portfolios from student work folders.

* * * *

Have you ever seen a blue crab molt its shell? First it retreats from deep water, rich with life's energy, to muck around in soft wet sand or marsh grass until it finds its berth for shedding. A small crack opposite its eyes breaks the bond between the crab's upper and lower shell. As its body absorbs water and expands, the break in the shell opens further, thus widening the path of escape. Pushing and pulling, squirming and stretching, the crab struggles to shed its shell, struggles to grow. Sometimes it even loses a claw or leg, starting a new process within the growth process. Inside the crab's new shell, new legs grow until the next molting, when a different crab emerges, a crab in which oldness and newness are one.

Slowly but surely, as surely as the blue crab sheds its shell, my second grade students and I found a freshness of learning, struggled with our uniqueness, and enjoyed our successes. Writing led us to discover the cracks in our shells as we drafted and shared, revised and shared, reflected and celebrated, celebrated our writing and celebrated our growth. We were writers and we were thinkers. Through portfolio development and assessment we had changed, we knew we had changed, and we knew how we had changed.

No More One-Shots

Jane Juska

*A California teacher wants portfolios to free her
students from grades, teacher dependence, and
"one-shot" writing assignments. She discovers
the potential of portfolios to accomplish at least
two of these goals.*

It seemed like a good idea then. "Then" was in August when
I decided that senior English would be different this time around.
This time we would do away with one-shots: no more "When do
we get our papers back, how much is the next one worth, where's
the wastebasket?" No more, "Well, that's it for comparison/
contrast, what's next?" Nope. This year we would work in a
continuum. "Continuum" sounds good. "Fits and starts" best
describes most of my teaching. "Continuum," now that's smooth.
"Meaningful continuum," how about that? Except for the damage
done to "meaningful" by an earlier decade, the phrase would
work. What I was thinking was that one piece of writing would
build upon the last, would give way to a new piece that would
build upon the last; the writing would exist in this continuum.
What I meant by "meaningful" was that each piece of writing
would become important to each student writer; it would not get
thrown away; it would be worked on, the Entire Semester. And it
would get collected by the writer into a portfolio. Finally—and if
this isn't meaningful, I don't know what is—I would do away with
grades. No grades, just teacher (me) and students (them) collabo-
rating in the classroom to perfect craft, approach art. Why did it
take me so long to think this up?

Maybe it was those grades that drove me to new heights of creativity. I hate grades, and I don't care if they're numbers or checks or checks with pluses, or As or Fs and then you translate them into numbers and find the average. It seems to me that throughout my years of teaching, no matter how many changes for the better I have attempted, any benefit derived therefrom is mitigated, if not canceled out, by the presence of grades. Now, this very year, we could write an Emancipation Proclamation for our time. "How many points is this worth?" the kids always asked. Portfolios will free us from grades, from servitude to an undeserving master!

Back in August, as I pondered this escape to freedom, I figured that, in the absence of grades, the kids would write for their writing groups, rewrite for those groups, and in the end, write for themselves in whose heads their writing groups would now rest. I would be the last resort. I would read their drafts, yes. I would indicate whether they were substantial enough to be designated Works in Progress. If so, I would plop "WP" on the papers, write suggestions and remarks, and hand the papers back the following half-hour. As the semester wore on, I would read and respond to their drafts both in writing and in conference. We would work as colleagues, the students and I, not antagonists. Our activity would be meaningful in the truest sense: No more one-shots, no more hostile grade-grabbers. And no more nights sitting at my desk, trying to stay awake while I devised yet another way to defend the grade I was placing on the paper. "What is the difference between a C and a C+?" some kid always asks. And, if I switch to numbers, "What is the difference between an 86 and an 89?"

Freed from the tyranny of the gradebook, the kids would no longer write for me. Down through the ages of my teaching, the refrain has rung out: "Just tell us what you want"; later, they demand I *tell* them what I want, and finally they complain, "If you had just *told* us what you wanted in the first place ..." The sentence completed would read, "... then we could have all gotten As." They continue, "So it's your fault, not that you're not a nice person and all, but maybe you should think about using the overhead projector like Mr. McElhare last year. Whenever he gave an assignment, he would write on the overhead exactly what we should have in the paper. I really learned in his class."

Portfolios will save us. They will save us from becoming embroiled in meaningless go-and-stop tasks whose end is to appease Boss Teacher, empowered by her gradebook to slay or merely to wound.

In September, we come face-to-face. They scare me, these seniors who are determined, even desperate, to go to college. At seventeen, they are not fooling around anymore. They want a first semester GPA that will impress all the college admissions boards in the country. They'll do what they have to in order to get it. Safe at home, I write them a letter. Back at school, head tucked into my Dickensian collar, eyes lowered, I hand it out, and tiptoe over to the corner of the room where I pretend to enter meaningful lessons into my Lesson Plan book. Here is part of that letter:

> *Portfolios due at the end of the semester. No grades till quarter time and those only a report of progress, then no grades again till semester. Semester grade based on the quality of work included in the portfolio. Why, you are asking. Why can't we do like always: hand in papers and get comments back and grades and then we'll know how we're doing and we won't have to worry and wonder if we're passing and what're we supposed to tell our parents, huh? Why can't this class be like my seventh grade English class which was my favorite ...*

> *Now, calm down. You and I will work our ways through different kinds of writing, different kinds of literature. You will give me drafts of your writing, the record of which I will keep in my gradebook, and I will comment on the drafts with an eye to helping you revise. You'll be writing comparison/contrast papers, definition papers, argumentative papers, personal experience/reflective papers, stories, poems — and you'll be re-writing them to get some or all of them ready for the portfolio. You will be learning and re-learning through-*

out the semester, and in the end you will put together a demonstration of your proficiencies in writing and in understanding and appreciating literature. That demonstration we will call a portfolio. You will be proud of it.

At the end of the letter, I ask them to write back to me. I expect an explosion. What I get are responses like "Well, it sounds ok," "Sorta different," "Why not." These seniors may be less frightening than I had imagined, but they are also less excited about this than I had hoped. They'll see, though; it'll happen. This very September, all will be different. We will dive into the meaningful continuum where all swimming will be downstream with a few rapids along the way to keep things interesting.

September whips across August like Hurricane Andrew. In the classroom, for six whole weeks, from September well into October, nobody hands in any drafts. We write these little starters in class. The kids put them in their writing folders. Come writing group day, they get out the starters they like best and — they talk. Writing group days become talking group days. Why trouble themselves with this writing stuff, they wonder. They are floating, adrift, yet comfortably moored to the shore of the classroom. With no pressure, no deadlines, no threats, only pleas from a single source — me — why not bob up and down as long as the weather lasts? Oh, I can talk about writing as discovery, as learning, as art, and I do. My audience is the moon, a moon not ready to turn the tide.

Ok, end of October, end of first quarter, grades to the parents. Fortunately, I remember this period of accountability before the entire eight weeks have gone by. In September, I had written this terrific argumentative essay for the class, assuming that, just as in the old days, the go-for-the-grade days, the kids would write one, too. They didn't. Until now, when I get them to agree that, yes, they should argue for their own quarter grades and that, yes, the argumentative essay they had complimented me on might now be helpful to them as well. And whoops! There seems to be no basis, such as work attempted or completed, for arguing for an A or even a C! The work begins to get done. Drafts appear on writing group days. Drafts begin to come into me. And some truly fine argumentative papers get written.

The problem is that they are writing for a grade, not a grade that will get sent to colleges, not one they will talk about with their friends. This grade is for parents; in many cases, the ease with which their home lives will proceed depends on this grade. Much as I wish, I cannot abolish grades altogether. Much as I hate to admit it, not much progress has been made toward getting kids to write for the sake of writing/learning/thinking. Am I more naive than I thought?

We Confront Grades

Yes. It is naive to believe that people who have been in school for twelve years will, in their twelfth year, become learners for the sake of learning. The kids speak fondly of those early elementary school years when teachers' comments replaced grades, where parent-teacher conferences replaced report cards. But by seventh grade at least, reality hits and yes, they will tell you, they do what they have to do in school for whatever grade they need to get. Be realistic, they insist; our GPAs determine our futures.

In November, at the beginning of the second quarter, I reintroduce the portfolio, this time focusing not at all on the result of all this, the portfolio itself. This time, I describe what I envision happening with their writing as it grows and changes. "Your writing group will offer suggestions. You will revise accordingly or not, as you see fit. You will give it to me. I will offer encouragement and suggestions." My tone is comforting, reassuring, avuncular (auntular?). "Take a look at all those Works in Progress you've got in your folders and pull out one you like well enough to do some work on." Pamela, her face contorted with worry and frustration, cries out, "But what if what we like doesn't fit the assignment?" "What assignment?" says Darren. "The only assignment is the portfolio. We can choose what goes in it." "But," — Pamela has learned to be assertive though not attractively so — "she said in that letter she gave us back in September we had to write comparison and contrast, like that." Michelle, whose intelligence I am only now coming to appreciate, answers, "She said we would be *doing* that writing. And we have, if you look in your folder. She didn't say that's the only stuff that could go in!" Michelle's impatience is beautiful to behold. I nod. "So let me get this straight," says Tim. "We decide what can go in the portfolio. So we can use the stuff like the argumentative and the comparison and contrast and the definition — those beginnings? Those WPs, if we want?" I nod. "But we can fix them up?" I nod. "So." Mark sits, arms crossed over his bench-pressed chest, chin jutting into the space beyond, eyes focused some five inches over my head. "What you're saying is that we could write three or four or even five drafts of the same paper. Right?" I nod. "Can we do some of this stuff in class?" I nod. He uncrosses his arms, shuffles through his WPs, and says, "I got work to do. Can we start now?" I nod up and down, quickly, definitely, eagerly, enthusiastically. Pamela glares balefully in my direction.

We See If It Flies

It is only now that our classroom begins to approach what Nel Noddings says school should be: "... places in which teachers and students live together, talk to each other, reason together, take delight in each other's company. " Pamela's scowl notwithstanding, we read to each other from *Great Expectations*, talk about the times and people in our own lives that Pip and friends remind us of. We write in class; the kids show their drafts to their writing groups. Then they show them to me. We sit together at my desk or theirs, talking about the writing. Every time I get a draft, I ooh and aah, take it home and comment lavishly and helpfully on it, and Get It Back The Next Day! Gradually, the trickle becomes a flow. And although the drafts go through the writing groups, primarily because I insist, ultimately they come to me. Post-Its become big time in my classroom. Those little yellow devils stick to each draft. They grin up at me. They read like this: "First draft. See if it flies." "Please revise. Is the argument strong enough? Any more facts that I should include in essay?" "Second draft, Is it better?" "2nd draft, I know 2nd para. needs work, but see if the rest is ok." "Every comment you can think of, please say. I want all the help I can get."

This is not right. What made me think this portfolio thing would help them write for themselves, each other? The closer we get to the end of the semester, the more drafts appear on my desk; Post-Its wave demandingly from their surfaces. "Fix this." "This is my first draft. Now what?" Pamela, not one to be left behind, buys her own stapler so she can affix one draft to another, so that her stack of papers (and ultimately her portfolio; Pamela thinks ahead) will outweigh everybody else's. She buys new boxes of Ritz crackers each week, tries out the peanut butter Ritzes, goes on to Ho-Hos. By the year's end, Pamela herself will have gained a good twenty pounds, one for each draft. She will outweigh us all.

Kids stop me in the hall between classes. "You're gonna love my next draft." They wave drafts at me from across the quad. "Get ready!" they warn, proud grins smearing their faces. "It's number four!"

Everybody Knows
You're the One to Come to

Monica drags this stranger of a kid into class. "This is Joshua. He's got a draft of a story and he wants to know if you'd read it and make suggestions for revision." I stare indignantly at the two of them. Monica continues, "Everybody knows you're the one to come to."

I have dreams. In them, Shannon, readying her portfolio even while I sit next to her, drowns. The principal and I jump off a cliff. I arrive to teach a class; it is not there; I cannot find it; it is my fault. I run to catch a plane, too late, my fault.

Is this ridiculous or what? Even my unconscious is telling me I have made a mistake. The kids' writing belongs to me; they gave it to me; they expect me to fix it the way I want it; they are beginning to like this revision process; finally, they are finding out what I want. They are coming to me *more* than ever, not *less*! I have made the juices of life sweeter! This nectar I have so unknowingly concocted is making these children stronger and healthier! But when — and how — do I put wormwood on the dug? I am running dry. And they need to be out and about finding their own food, no matter how difficult the search.

What is my part in all this? I have this discussion with my friend Susan who has been using portfolios in her classes for a long time. "But Susan," I whine, "I know a lot about writing. Is it fair for me to withhold my expertise?" Susan sighs and says totally unhelpful things like "I can't answer that question." Susan is wise. She understands that I will have to work out my own answers, that borrowing hers will be just that: borrowing hers. But I do know, from our discussions, that Susan insists that her students solicit friends, family, significant others as readers of their portfolios. She sees her role as facilitating the process, as active *in medias res*, not in judging the merit of the final product. Well, I'm going to try that. Next semester.

But it is still this semester. It is January, presentation day. Portfolios are due. Here they come. Pamela has watercolored a forest scene for her cover. Later, when they fall into my computer, I will discover that Kristen has added confetti to the pages of her portfolio — "to make it extra nice," she writes on the inside cover. All the portfolios arrive with letters of introduction that explain what the portfolios intend to demonstrate. Each piece in the portfolio lies beneath its own cover letter; it explains the process the writer went through and estimates the strengths and weaknesses of the piece.

I call in sick and, at home in front of my computer, go into a trance. I read and read and write and write. It's fun. My responses are not terribly lengthy; they do not point the writer to revision; all that's behind us. For the most part, I applaud and, occasionally, despair. In the end, I come up with a grade for the entire portfolio and so the semester. I base the grade on the quality of the writing, the number of revisions of those original pieces. I figure in, sort of, the number of works in progress we have shared over the semester. Pamela's portfolio is thickest. She gets a B. Why not an A, she will want to know. I bubble the grade onto the Scantron. Grades are back in town.

Before I return their portfolios to them, I write and deliver another letter. (I write letters to them frequently, agreeing with them that the sound of teachers' voices palls somewhere around the tenth grade.) In it, I ask them to write back about the process of putting together this portfolio. "At the end of *Great Expectations*," I write, "Pip becomes a true gentleperson by having a loving heart. Has anything happened to you during your journey?" Here is what I discover:

- Not everybody loved portfolios.

   Anonymous: *As seniors we don't want to be writing papers all year long. We have to write enough when we're sending in our applications, to college.*

   Shannon: *Personally, I don't think my grade in this class shows what kind of student I am. I feel I am much more knowledgable than a crummy old D.*

   Dan: *It's like being in a prisoner camp, not knowing when you'll die, or even if you will die at all. I think we have completely shyed away from learning our basic English skills such as, how to write an essay, vocabulary (being that there are always new words out there to learn), and grammar.*

   Cambie: *One thing I really disliked about the portfolio were revisions. I'm not really into 2, 3 and even 4 drafts.*

   Pamela: *It's hard for me to float for 9 weeks praying I'll get an A or a B. I don't like arguing for my grade.*

- Some offered grudging acceptance.

   Ryan: *Portfolios and I don't get along, thank you. But we can work together when necessary. I don't like rewriting things, but if I am forced to, then I (reluctantly) will.*

- Some reflected on the process.

   Debra: *Every day I wrote and revised and cursed the paper I wrote on. I tried harder than I ever had…*

Medina: *Drafts had to be written, revisions had to be made, conferences with Ms. Juska had to be scheduled and worst of all, the easy A vanished from our dreams.*

• Some learned.

Tim: *The main thing the portfolio taught me about myself was that my study habits draw water through a straw. I've always put things off to the last minute. However, with my portfolio, this was different. I didn't wait until the last minute except for one piece. And guess what? This was the piece in the portfolio that I received the lowest grade on. Surprise, surprise.*

Lisa: *I liked having conferences with you, and turning in drafts at our own pace and getting back comments. I also found that revision is a really important key to a good paper. Some of my papers changed drastically and some didn't. It was interesting.*

• Some said exactly what I wanted to hear.

Michelle: *Getting a grade on every paper I turned in had ceased to matter. All I needed/wanted was comments and critiques. I learned that senior English doesn't need a vocab. test every week or grades on every paper.*

Misty: *As a person who constantly moniters grades and deadlines this was frightening. I had to learn to discipline myself and revise without red letters staring up at me from off the paper. At the beginning of this semester, and even this quarter, I lacked confidence in my ability to write anything well. ... I never believed that I would be able to achieve an A.* [She did.] *This portfolio taught me discipline and self-reliance. These tools will be very beneficial to me in college, where you don't have teachers breathing down your neck.*

Carole: *When you turn in a portfolio, it's like turning in a small piece of your life and soul. It gets to the point where you write more for yourself and not for grading purposes only.*

The Meaningful Continuum

My kids' responses tell me that, while not everyone is happy, we just might have created a meaningful continuum. And grades? I would like to give that responsibility over to a peer reader, or to the writing groups, since we do spend time in class developing criteria by which to evaluate writing. But I can't. Maybe I'm too old. Which may be the point. I am too old to be nursing young people whose teeth get progressively sharper. I will have to find a better way. So second semester I try this: I require two readers, one within the class, one without. The readers will write their impressions. I will read them, along with the cover letters accompanying each piece, and make my final evaluation accordingly.

It is true that, over this long haul, I've said everything I could say about the pieces. But again, now in June, having called in sick, I sit at my desk at home and listen to the whir of my Mac waiting to record my responses, minimal let us hope. Shelley has included a poem about young love. I thought I let my opinion of young love poems be known long ago. Wait a minute. The girl in this one grows up. And in the cover letter, in which Shelley explains the inspiration of her poem, she writes that she has decided to have the baby and to keep it. What?! I turn to Shelley's friend's comments, the friend outside of class Shelley has asked to read her portfolio. The friend's name is Mindy. Mindy writes that after reading Shelley's portfolio, she too has decided to keep her baby, despite advice to the contrary.

I turn off my computer and phone Susan. She is at home reading portfolios. We exchange stories. She tells me about Livia who rushed into class, late, portfolio in hand. Livia explains her lateness: "My daddy was shot last night." We wonder together about the importance of anything we are doing: these portfolios, these grades, this responding, this revising. Nel Noddings has this to say:

> [W]hen schools focus on what really matters in life, the
> cognitive ends we are now striving toward in such painful
> and artificial ways will be met as natural culminations of the
> means we have wisely chose (p. 169).

I don't know. Maybe it is in the very nature of school not to focus on "what really matters in life." Maybe it is the nature of teachers to overlook, to avoid, to ignore. Susan and I listen to each other's silence, then, in the absence of anything better, return to the portfolios. There, the kids come alive through the letters they have written, through the poems and stories and essays they have done. Whether or not I am ready or willing or able, the writing does indeed focus on "what really matters." It occurs to me that I ought to be grateful to come this close to participating in the creative act. For too long in my teaching career I tried to maintain a distance, believing that professionalism lay somewhere in that space between the kids and me. Portfolios do not allow for distance. They compel both writer and reader into an intimacy not necessarily wished for by either party, an intimacy which will change, for better or for worse, the participants, an intimacy which will surprise, delight, disappoint and even frighten. No wonder I am exhausted. No wonder I will be ready for another go-around.

Reference

Noddings, N. (1991). Stories in dialogue: Caring and interpersonal reasoning. In C. Witherell & N. Noddings (Eds.), *Stories lives tell: Narrative and dialogue in education* (pp. 157-170). New York: Teachers College Press.

Portfolios in a Fifth Grade Classroom

Nancy Green

A Missouri teacher describes the evolution of portfolio assessment in her classroom and the rubric she developed with her students. Her goal is to help students become better writers and, at the same time, to keep the paper load from overwhelming the teacher.

The right form of portfolio assessment for my fifth graders evolved over the first year we experimented with a writing workshop. This assessment in its final form met my needs as an evaluator and worked as a motivation for my students to write and keep on writing.

I began a writing workshop in the fifth grade by setting aside one whole hour in an already full daily schedule. The first ten minutes of that hour were for a mini-lesson. This lesson could be on a language or writing skill many of the children needed. It could be a beautiful piece of writing I wanted the children to experience and emulate. It could be a writing workshop rule or guideline that we needed to work out or clarify.

After the ten minute mini-lesson, students wrote for forty minutes on topics of their choice. During this time I moved around the classroom talking to children about what they were writing. The last ten minutes of each workshop were devoted to time for those who wanted to read aloud something they had written.

During the first couple of weeks of writing workshop I felt so swamped with the mechanics of just getting started that I did not even want to think about evaluation. I wanted to do the easiest possible thing for a while. I thought the minimum I could do was one grading per week.

I said to my thirty novice writers, "Friday I want you to be ready to hand in one piece of writing. The grade I put on this piece will be your language grade for the week. Pick out from your week's work what you think will give you the best grade."

A Realistic Way to Assess Writing Workshop

This might work, I thought. I can't possibly put a grade on everything the children are writing, but I have to figure out some realistic way to assess what we are accomplishing in writing workshop. I will only have to take home one stack of papers on one night a week. This leaves me free to participate in writing workshop without worrying about assessment. I graded one piece of writing from all thirty children every Friday night for about three weeks before I realized the evaluation system was not going to work. I was reading a piece written by Tasha. The piece was interesting and well written. It easily deserved a 100%.

The problem was that Tasha had done nothing else all week except this one piece of writing. She had chatted with Donna during one workshop. She had spent one day working on an art project. If I put 100% on Tasha's paper, would she feel free to waste her writing time again next week? Probably.

I put a 70% at the top of the paper thinking, Tasha is not going to be happy with this grade, and neither am I. It is the best grade I can give her, though, knowing how little time she spent on this piece of writing.

Sure enough, as soon as I handed papers back on Monday, Tasha was at my side lamenting, "Mrs. Green, I think this piece was worth more than 70%!"

"I agree with you, Tasha," I answered. "This is easily a 100% paper, but remember last week when you spent one whole workshop chatting and another workshop on an art project? When I graded your paper, I had to take that into account. This grade is not for this paper alone but for what you did in writing workshop all last week."

Tasha was obviously confused. My explanation was too abstract for her. If she could write a 100% paper, then she wanted that paper to have a 100% even if it took only one day for her to write it. I had to either start grading everything the children wrote or consider some kind of portfolio assessment. Clearly, it was time to develop something that the children and I could understand and live with for the rest of the year.

I needed an assessment that would motivate my students to do a lot of writing. I wanted them to learn to spend their time in writing workshop wisely and not fritter it away chatting or doing other projects. I wanted an assessment that would foster the self-discipline every writer needs.

I also wanted an assessment that would not require hours of my time. After all, writing workshop was only one hour in the day, and I had six other subjects to teach and grade. Going to a portfolio assessment where I evaluated as a whole everything the children had written for the week seemed the only feasible solution.

I knew it was imperative for the children to understand and approve whatever assessment we used for writing workshop. Otherwise, they would view it as a "teacher thing," something for which they didn't have to be responsible. I wanted my students to "own" their assessment just as they did their writing. I decided that the way to meet our needs was to ask the class to help me decide what should be graded in writing workshop.

Quality of Writing

I began our next workshop by discussing Tasha's dissatisfaction with her week's grade. Heads began to nod all around the room. I had everyone's attention. Other students had gotten grades which they didn't understand or with which they didn't agree. I wrote on the board "Quality of Writing" and said, "This is what I think is most important in your writing. This means you have written something interesting to your reader and something your reader can understand. We will have 100 points every week for writing workshop. I think Quality of Writing should get 25 of those points. Now, you decide what else should get points."

The discussion that followed was serious and heated. The children knew exactly on what they wanted to be graded, and we went with their choices.

They decided on 25 points for paying attention during mini-lessons (I never would have thought of this one), 25 points for the amount of writing in their folders each week, and 25 points for hard work — no wasted time — during writing workshop. This gave us a rubric we could all understand and agree on for our weekly portfolio assessment.

I devised a grade sheet that had five headings down the left of the paper: Quality of Writing, Attention, How Much Writing, Hard Work, Total. Across the top of the grade sheet, I put each Friday's date. Every student got their sheet on Friday. They put the sheet in their portfolios and handed them in to me.

I carried all the folders home Friday evening. I took about forty-five minutes to go through them and put the grades on the grade sheets. This did not really require much reading because I had been reading and discussing pieces with children all week during workshop. I had a pretty good idea what each folder contained before I even opened it.

On Monday I handed back portfolios. The children took out their grade sheets, added up their points, and handed the grade sheets back to me. This evaluation system took only a few minutes of class time, leaving my students' precious writing time intact. I thought carrying home thirty portfolios every Friday was a small price to pay for an evaluation system that would motivate my students to write.

I was working on the premise that the more writing my students did, the better writers they would become. Therefore, I expected to see lots of writing in each portfolio every week. I wanted my students to feel free to use their workshop time in whatever way they chose. They could spend time in discussion or drawing (both valid prewriting activities for some writers) if they wanted. However, if children took advantage of this classroom freedom, they had to do writing outside of workshop in order to have enough writing to get a good grade.

It took a couple of weeks for all the children to understand how much writing they were going to have to do each week to get the kind of grade they wanted. The first week I handed back portfolios with grade sheets I got some arguments from students who had been butterflying around during workshop time. Arguments usually came from especially bright children who were used to not having to expend much effort to get good grades.

Students and Teacher
Negotiate for Grades

Arguments would go like this one from Will, one of my most gifted writers: "Mrs. Green, you only gave me 60 points for last week! How come?"

"Yes, Will," I replied stopping at his desk. "Show me what you had in your portfolio for me to grade this week."

After some shuffling of various papers which should have been cleaned out of his folder and filed, Will came up with one poem, eight lines, and one half-finished story, two pages.

"You said this poem was an excellent piece of writing," Will argued, gearing up his defense. "You said it had good describing words. Everyone liked it when I read it out loud last week."

"Yes, this poem is very good writing. That's why I gave you 25 points for Quality of Writing. You also paid attention during every mini-lesson last week, so I gave you another 25 points for that. This half-finished story was in your folder last Friday, so it doesn't count for this week. I can only give you 5 points for How Much Writing because you only have eight lines of writing here. I can only give you 5 points for Hard Work because if you had worked hard this folder would be full. If you do not get busy writing, I will not be as generous with points this week as I was last week."

Will fumed and pouted, but he got busy writing. This was assessment he could understand even if he didn't want to agree with it. Knowing he would have a low grade if his portfolio was not full of writing forced Will to discipline himself and be responsible for how he used his writing workshop time. The next time Will handed me his portfolio, it had eight poems, two finished stories, one play, and a commercial.

I took one more mini-lesson time to make sure everyone understood what I was looking for in portfolios. I wanted to make sure the children understood how hard they would have to work to do as much writing as I knew they were capable of doing.

We were three-fourths of the way through the year when I decided I had to change our assessment program one more time. I started to the car one Friday night with portfolios and almost couldn't make it because they were so heavy.

"These kids are writing so much in a week that I can't carry it all home!" I complained to myself. "Isn't that just like a teacher?" I chuckled. Evaluate the kids on how much they write and then gripe because they write so much you can't carry it.

Solving the Paper Load and Increasing Student Writing

This was a problem that was easily solved. The next Friday when writing workshop began, I said, "Tonight I will not be taking any portfolios home. I will be going through all your folders during this workshop time, so get them ready now. If you want to discuss your grade sheet, be at your desk when I get there. Otherwise, you go on with your writing while I look at your portfolios and do the grade sheets."

This worked so well I was surprised I had not thought of it sooner. Many children wanted to be at their desk to discuss their work with me. If I had a question or wanted to comment on particularly well-written pieces the child was close by. If a child wondered about something on the grade sheet, I was more than willing to negotiate and explain.

My fifth graders were amazed at how much writing they could do in one week. They began to see themselves as writers. They could point to their growing body of work to prove that they were writers. They felt good about what they were accomplishing in writing workshop.

The portfolio assessment my students and I devised encouraged and motivated the children to do the massive amounts of writing I wanted them to do. My premise that the more writing they did, the better writers they would become was correct. By the end of the year, the fifth graders were writing much more sophisticated and polished pieces, and they were better able to evaluate and edit their own and other people's writing. Not only had assessment encouraged students to write, it also had taught them to discipline themselves and take responsibility for their use of writing workshop time.

The portfolio assessment we used in our fifth grade became a valuable teaching and learning tool for all of us. I think this is assessment at its best, teacher and student evaluating so that each can improve and proceed with the writing process.

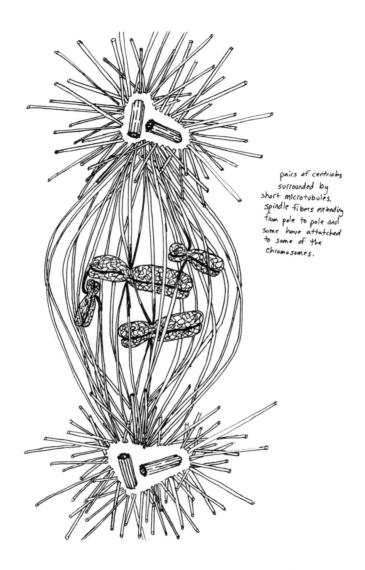

pairs of centrioles
surrounded by
short microtubules.
Spindle fibers extending
from pole to pole and
some have attached
to some of the
chromosomes.

Chad Smith

Portfolios in Biology

John Dorroh

A Mississippi science teacher revamps test taking in his biology class. Students assemble portfolios from a list of alternative assessment modes, including notebook entries, open-ended lab reports, photo essays, oral presentations, poetry, and collaborative group projects.

For fifteen years science students had suggested that my tests were not showing what they had learned about the various science concepts we had "covered." I easily identified with their feelings about multiple-choice and fill-in-the-blank assessment but did not have enough courage to tackle the problem. Finally during the 1991-92 school year, "Mr. D." (that's me) went out — way out — on a limb.

In this story I want to give as complete and honest an account as possible, giving credit where credit is due. My hat goes off to friend, neighbor, co-walker, and English teacher, Anne Wilson, who led me serendipitously to my first Writing Project workshop. It was a seven-day revival, led by my local National Writing Project site's co-directors, Sandra Burkett and Sherry Swain, blessed by the presence of my soon-to-be guru, Bob Tierney, a former California science teacher. And of course, it would be rather foolish of me to omit students such as Chad Smith, who helped make my transition possible.

Bob had become disenchanted with the accepted science teaching practices in his school and had become involved with the Bay Area Writing Project. Part of his metamorphosis into a unique writing-based science instructor evolved from classroom research with fellow teacher Harry Stookey. (Tierney, 1981)

I listed and participated in no fewer than twenty-five writing-in-science strategies in his three-day visit, including expressive writing with journals, Neuron Notes, class logs, free-form lab reports, and skits involving cell parts. I wrote hypotheses concerning temperature preferences of mealybugs and dabbled with the idea of having students write practice essays and their own codes of classroom ethics.

That single meeting with "Cousin Bob" served as the catalyst for my classroom overhaul. I returned to Room 23 at West Point High, a 750-student school, grades 9-10, in northeast Mississippi, with so many ideas that I thought I'd explode. (Looking back, I now realize that my biggest mistake that first year was trying to incorporate too much too soon.) Raw excitement prevented me from analyzing what it was that I wanted to accomplish. I should have given myself and my students more time to reflect. For example, why had the journal activities been so well received by my students? What element of skit-writing had made learning the concepts seem fun? And how would I get learners to reflect on their own progress?

Such questions in the beginning stages of my transition made me take a much closer look at my students. Who were they? Would they be willing to participate? How would the school environment affect their success in science class?

What were they going to do upon graduation?

A simple investigation revealed that most of the students in my advanced biology classes (80-90%) planned to attend college, and the majority of them had either a somewhat favorable impression of science, based on their former classes, or were indifferent to science. Many admitted that they were taking this particular class to meet college entrance requirements.

The Summer Institute, which I attended the following June, provided me with a theoretical framework upon which I began to build my own unique program of science teaching and learning. Response groups allowed me to engage in "hands-on" writing and revising. Reading the current literature helped me to validate my plans for the upcoming school year. All in all, the Institute pumped me up with confidence, revitalizing my soul, helping alleviate most of the guilt I had for abandoning my "old way," which included teacher-dominated lecturing/note-taking, canned laboratory "investigations," and multiple-choice assessments. I asked myself: What are my science students already doing that could be used in place of traditional tests? With the multitude of diverse activities that occurs in my science classes in a single week, compiling a working list of choices was not a difficult task. Seven kinds of activities dominated, including journaling, participating in small group work, investigating original problems in the lab, creating works of art, communicating with an audience in the form of oral reports and presentations, writing skits, plays, short stories, poems, and essays. (Taking traditional tests could still be an option for those who felt comfortable with that mode.) Using these seven "modes of evaluation" (see modes 1-4, Figure 1 below), I had created a menu. And it hit me like the proverbial ton of bricks that this menu was my new tool for assessing.

Figure 1

Students:

Below you will find your "menu" of choices for how you will be evaluated (graded) for the first nine-week grading period. As you can see, there are several choices. It is your responsibility to choose at least three modes of evaluation and to follow each protocol (set of guidelines) that accompanies each mode. Listen in class for any changes, which can occur without notice.

1. Journaling. (Expressive Mode Notebook)

* makes use of "Rules of Writing Practice" (mimeograph sheet; should have been placed as first page in EM)
* each new entry on clean page; entries longer than one page are continued on the back of the sheet
* entries to be numbererd; example: "Entry #3" (top of page)
* entry pages to bear the date; example: "8/21" (top of page)
* entry pages to bear the topic title; example: "Scientists" (top of page)
* entries to be more than ½ page in "regular-sized" handwriting
* entries should pose questions

2. Small-group work

* small group sessions must have a specific focus (goal/objective)
* small group sessions must produce a "product" (to be announced)

3. Written tests

* chapter tests, possible daily quizzes, etc. (All students must take the written nine-weeks exam and the state-mandated FLP quizzes.)

4. Drama, Fiction, Poetry, and Essay

* written and/or "acted-out" plays/skits relating to the content
* written fictional short stories that relate to content
* written poetry that relates to the content
* written essay that relate to the content

Uses of the Modes of Evaluation

We called journals "Expressive Mode" notebooks (EMs) and housed them in wildly decorated cardboard boxes on the floor. A typical week included two six-minute entries, topics assigned according to the subject being studied. Examples included "A Day in the Life of a Scientist," "Nutrition in America," or "All About Enzymes." Often I used simple prompts such as "The worst thing about using the scientific method is…" Upon student requests, we reserved Fridays for ten minutes of "free-write," or anything goes, not necessarily about science.

Small group work — stabs at collaborative learning — could be virtually anything: writing skits about how cell organelles interrelate, developing interview questions for an upcoming visit from some famous scientist, or preparing briefs for presentation to the Town Council in favor of locating a hazardous waste facility in an adjoining county.

Open-ended labs replaced highly-structured, canned "investigations." Students wrote lab reports to others than myself — to Michael Jackson, or to the local mayor, or parents, grandparents, boyfriends, girlfriends, and so on. Many were narrative instead of "follow-this-form," and this change seemed to free up my students, giving them the opportunity to experiment without restriction to my old traditional five-part report form.

Another mode catered to creative students who liked to express themselves artistically with cartoons, sketches, clay models, and photo-essays. Tenth-grader Chad Smith's impressive cartoon series (see opposite page) seemed to help convince many dubious colleagues that alternative forms of assessment in science are not only possible but useful.

Oral reports and presentations provided opportunities for those who enjoyed speaking in front of a group. We generated topics from the content we were studying , but topics could come from special interests, by prearrangment with me. Also, I insisted — demanded actually — that presenters communicate effectively with their audience.

Finally, students were free to pick drama, fiction, poetry, and essays or any combination thereof to meet the number of required

projects in the grading period. Once again, the specific content being studied served as a source for each writing project.

I found it especially interesting that even though tests (the objective type) were available for those who felt comfortable taking them, very few students chose that option (about 5-10%). I quickly assured one colleague, bothered that my students were not getting enough practice in test-taking, that they were indeed receiving more than enough practice in their other five classes.

Certain students, relatively few in number, such as Chad Smith, our resident artist-scientist, became my "barometer of sanity." Each time I began to feel that the aforementioned limb was going to break, Chad turned in yet another piece of art so content-related, so breathtaking that I felt instantly revitalized. And then one day it dawned on me (Aha!) in a fresh light: *Letting students decide how to be evaluated makes sense!* Why hadn't I done it sooner?

Just how does the menu work? What are the mechanics? How do you track progress and growth? What about grading? Where do portfolios fit in?

I handed students a menu and asked them to select a minimum of three modes of evaluation for the first nine-week grading period. I modeled all modes, showing as many samples as I could corral and, in general, painting as clear a picture as possible of expectations for each category. Any gray area was left open to student interpretation; this kept the process from becoming too predictable.

I insisted that students carefully assess their own particular strengths and weaknesses and choose menu items accordingly. It did not take me long to realize that many students might not know their strengths, since they lacked practice at this kind of self-assessment.

"Once you make selections," I said, "consider yourself locked in for the duration of the nine weeks." I drew up primitive contracts (see Figure 2 on opposite page) and students filled them out, disbelief on their faces when they saw that they really did not have to take those horrible traditional tests.

"There's got to be some catch," said Samantha.

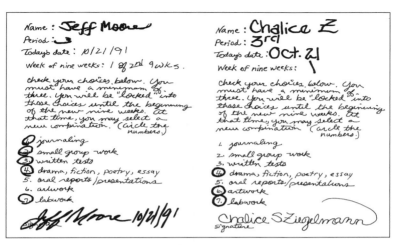

Figure 2

I smiled. "No, Samantha, no catch. What you sign up for is where your grade comes from. It's that simple."

Signing contracts emphasized the importance of making careful decisions and sticking to them. "If you feel that you have made some wrong choices," I told them, "you may re-select another combination at the beginning of the next nine weeks."

Next I constructed a class profile (see Figure 3 on next page) for each period and taped them to the back of the door. Not only did these profiles give a quick picture of the choices of the students in all five classes, but they were used for reference — for both teacher and student — when memory lapsed forced the inevitable, "Hey, I forgot what I signed up for."

I distributed deadline sheets to students who chose the writing cluster, artwork, and oral reports. Three or four deadlines loomed in each nine-week period, spaced out to prevent "project overload." Ten points per day was deducted from each numerical grade whenever a project was late, barring excused absences.

My science students demanded that a numerical grade be put on each and every project. I had a particularly distasteful time assigning such grades to pieces of artwork and poems. Hesitantly, I developed crude critique sheets for this purpose, realizing that this portion of the evaluation process would have to be

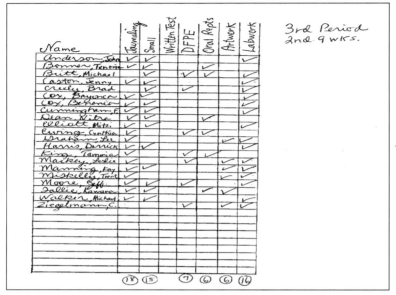

Figure 3

improved in the future. I also announced and welcomed one-on-one miniconferences to iron out any grade disputes.

My school board's grading policy stated that I must have at least eight grades for each student in each nine-week period and that a written nine-week exam be administered and counted as twenty-five per cent of the total grade. These guidelines proved to be satisfactory, and I had no problem with them.

All of my course content is built around required (and additional) objectives.

Integrating Portfolio Assessment

Designing and implementing this menu-selection process was no doubt a gigantic step for me both professionally and personally. However, I did not feel as if all the pieces of the picture were there.

Sandra Burkett and Sherry Swain, my local site co-directors (NWP), once again came to my rescue, inviting me to become part of a task force for implementing portfolio assessment in our state.

I immediately liked the idea but wasn't quite certain how I'd go about integrating the two projects. Being a risk-taker and a part-time crazy person, I accepted the invitation.

Several weeks before our first meeting in October, I met with a fellow teacher, an art teacher as a matter of fact, and asked, "Do you have a portfolio? Most artists have a portfolio, don't they? Let me see yours."

"I don't need a portfolio," she said. "I'm not trying to convince anyone to hire me." I think she could read the disappointment in my expression and changed tone rather quickly. "But sometimes my students have a public exhibition, and that's sort of like a portfolio, isn't it?"

"I suppose. Gee, I don't know." I took a sip of coffee. "Yes, I think you're absolutely right."

Libby asked me if I was thinking about letting my science students construct portfolios. "It's a very good idea," she said. "Letting children select their best works, letting them see growth. Makes perfectly good sense to me," she said smiling.

Libby helped me see that I had to have a purpose for the portfolios. That purpose — or at least the main one — would be to help students tear down their negative images about scientists.

After my first meeting with the task force in October, I had a much clearer idea of how portfolios could be used in my science classes. Still, it took several additional meetings before all of my questions and answers began to gel. Curious individuals, both in and out of the teaching profession, began to quiz me: Just what is a portfolio? How can a teacher decide how much it counts in grading or should it be graded at all? Will it present more work for the teacher? How do the students store their works-in-progress? What if the students won't participate? Are portfolios just another bandwagon? I liked the questions very much. But I had trouble with comfortable answers. "We'll just have to wait and see," I often said.

The mechanics of assembling portfolios in my science classes proved successful. I told students to save everything they did; next I distributed plain manila folders to each one. I took photo-graphs of all those who consented, some preferring to bring photos from home, others drawing self-portraits. These were taped to the front of the folders along with large cartoon bubbles. "Inside these bubbles," I said, "write a couple of lines of text that describe how you feel about being a scientist." Pictures and text made the portfolios user-friendly and less threatening.

Approximately every three weeks I invited students to "play" for an entire class period with their portfolios-in-the-making. Each of these sessions was prefaced with a directive to reflect. For example, "If you had to pick three items in your portfolio to show to the Portfolio King in order to save your meager life, which three items would you pick and why?" Students were free to discuss their reflections with others, including me.

The one-hundred-plus folders were stored in my school-green filing cabinet. Rarely did they leave the room. If misplaced, how could a student replace such valuable documents?

Students began to "get the hang of it" during the last nine-week grading period. (Don't they always?) I noticed that they began asking for more time. At first I kidded them about being overly worried about the fact that the portfolios counted one-fourth of their last nine-week grade. But I could see in their faces and hear in their comments that they enjoyed working on them. All in all, I felt pretty good about the results.

Now that I have lived through one whole school year of menu selection coupled with portfolio assessment, I feel more confident to repeat the process, making changes, of course, where needed. Students so often are my best sources of criticism. "Don't wait so long to get started," said Phi. "Your critique sheets need to be improved," said Lashawn. And one of my own suggestions is to have more time — much more time — for student reflection.

How did other students feel about portfolios?

Kesheenia M. *The work in the portfolio helped me a lot. For instance, I discovered that I have a problem with my wording, and I'll do better.*

Reginald E. *It's another way to show how the student is progressing without using test scores... It is also a fun way to prove to yourself that you are progressing even when it does not seem like you are.*

Tom C. *It helps students to become responsible. This class made me learn responsibility, not always relying on the teacher to do something.*

Toyar G. *Doing a portfolio was hard work, but it was kind of neat. It's nice to sit back and look at all of your work.*

Al Q. *Revision is an important part of being a scientist.*

Marilyn E. *They made me believe that I need to improve my writing skills.*

Regina R. *Well, using portfolios in biology was unusual. I never did anything like that before. It required so much work. You had to make sure it was okay before you turned it in.*

Felisia H. *Is this portfolio idea a college thing?*

In Conclusion

It all began with listening to students say that tests were not measuring progress. I believed but I ignored for such a long time. And then one day, supported by the philosophies of writing-based instruction, I decided to take a giant risk.

What evolved was a system for science teaching and learning that allowed students the freedom to choose, the necessity to become responsible and accountable for their own classroom destiny, and a record of their best efforts. What could be more rewarding for any classroom teacher or student, regardless of subject matter?

Casting My Net

Tamsie West

A Mississippi teacher looks back on her first year of portfolio assessment, the decisions and roadblocks and unexpected lessons. She explores the dilemma of finding the time for portfolios and everything else too.

I thought I had botched the whole thing, had cast my nets and come up empty, but, in retrospect, maybe I haven't after all. I have just read my end of the year "What have you learned?" journals again. Although I read them when they came in, time-distance has given me a new perspective. Repeatedly my students have said that I have helped them to gain independence — that they learned to take responsibility for their work, that they feel confident enough now to say what they think and not what they think the teacher wants to hear. In part, their reactions have grown from the writing-process environment I try to establish in all my classes, an environment that includes establishing trust between students and between students and teacher, recognizing that "good writers don't get it right the first time," and writing lots of first draft pieces that receive consideration only on content. But in one class in particular, my fourth period Advanced English IV class, I might attribute that growth to the establishment of the portfolio as a self-evaluation tool.

In August 1991 I started work in a new school — again. Because my husband is a football coach, a profession almost as mobile as the armed services and the Methodist ministry, I had taught in four Mississippi schools before this one. I often joked with my Writing Project colleagues that I was the traveling evangelist for our group, spreading Writing Project ideas wherever I went. When we moved to the Jackson, Mississippi, area so that my husband could become head coach and athletic director at McLaurin High School, I looked carefully for a school that I thought would provide me with new opportunities for professional growth. And, after a fortunate conversation with a fellow Writing Project teacher, I found myself teaching senior English and Advanced Placement at Forest High School, a 600-student rural school (medium-sized by Mississippi standards) in the town of Forest in central Mississippi, about a fifty-minute commute from my new home. The student body at Forest High is racially balanced, with about sixty percent minority students; most of the students are from working-class or non-working families. The chicken processing plants are the major industries in town; when the school windows are open, the breeze wafts in with an unmistakable bouquet from the plant right down the street.

I received an invitation in September from the Mississippi Writing/Thinking Institute to be a member of a statewide portfolio task force designed to pilot staff development in using portfolios as an alternate assessment. When I read it I knew immediately that I had to say yes. It was a chance not only to work again with a devoted group of Writing Project teachers with whom I had collaborated often before, but also to make a difference in an area about which I had been concerned for some time — the apparent futility of attempting to assess whole language learning with standardized multiple choice tests. Besides, I had just begun something I was calling a portfolio in all my classes, and I was drowning. Somehow I didn't quite have the hang of what a portfolio should contain. I needed help.

After meeting for the first time with this task force in October at Mississippi State University and finding out that I really didn't know what portfolios were after all, I decided to pursue the portfolio process in only one class. I chose it because, at that time, it was giving me the least trouble in what was proving to be an arduous year. I didn't want to continue the hesitancy and shakiness of something new with kids who were having difficulty adjusting to my methods in the first place.

Focus on Student Autonomy

From that first meeting I had my "focus," an element that Mary Ann Smith of the National Writing Project had convinced task force members was an absolute essential. When I thought about what she said, of course, she made perfect sense. It was silly to start out on a road if you didn't at least have either an idea of where you wanted to go or some reason for traveling there, even if it were just to enjoy the sunshine. So I settled on my "focus": the portfolios in my classroom would establish student autonomy, get students to reflect on growth in writing and thinking skills, and celebrate student achievement. Other task force participants chose goals that fit the particular needs of their classrooms as well.

But, when I returned to school, I was unwilling to throw out lesson plans and units that I had established already, and they allowed little room for anything else. This year, perhaps because it was my first at a new school, students in all my classes displayed confusion about almost anything I attempted. With this senior class I obviously had to provide much more structure and guidance than usual, and so I had been careful to tell them what they could expect to be doing for the rest of the semester. I feared that "throwing the baby out with the bath water" would simply result in more chaos.

In addition, I still thought that portfolio pieces had to be "finished" pieces of writing, and we hadn't done enough of those to provide a truly representative sample. I didn't know how we were going to do more finished pieces. To take a piece of writing completely through prewriting, drafting, group response, revision, more group response, group editing, proofreading, and final copy takes days of class time. My principal already was hinting strongly that I wasn't pushing hard enough and that I was not "covering" enough material. And I felt guilty, too. After all, if I didn't get moving we weren't even going to finish the Elizabethan period, much less anything beyond the sixteenth century. Besides, the group that I had chosen for the portfolio work was supposed to be an advanced class.

So I went back in and attempted to undo all that I had said about portfolios at the beginning of the year when I didn't know what I was talking about. Then I superimposed the portfolio process on what I was teaching already — giving up two days, grudgingly, to compile portfolios consisting of five pieces of writing, three that would reflect student growth in writing skills over time, one "favorite" and one "best," although they had few "finished" pieces to choose from.

An Audience of Teachers

I told the students that I would be taking these portfolios to a meeting of some of the best teachers in the state, explained what the task force wanted to accomplish, and informed them that these educators were eager to see what we were doing in our classroom. I assured them that students from other schools around Mississippi were compiling portfolios, too, and that they were helping teachers change education in our state. They seemed anxious to participate in a project of this magnitude.

Letting them work with peers on their selections, I then asked them to reflect on each piece individually by writing about why they selected it and what they thought the work revealed about themselves as thinkers and writers. They acted confused at first, but soon appeared to be very busy. Knowing that other teachers would read and comment on their work made them eager to do their best. I stayed out of the procedure as much as possible, eavesdropping on groups from my corner. They seemed to know what I expected them to do.

When I asked for a general cover letter that would tell readers what they could learn about that student as a writer and thinker from the total portfolio, several students grumped that they had already covered that material in their individual reflections, and griped that they didn't want to think about those pieces any more. In the end, this complaint turned out to be a persistent one.

After the portfolio process was "over" (a ridiculous concept I now know, but that was the way I thought of it) we went back to everything else we were doing, and I took the portfolios they had compiled to the November meeting of the task force. When I first got a chance to contemplate the students' portfolios and their reflections, the superficiality of their meditations and selections disheartened me, and I reproached myself for not devoting more class time to those topics. However, I later discovered that shallow reflections had plagued almost all task force members. On November 5, I wrote in my teacher's log/journal:

After looking at the portfolios other teachers brought today I feel a lot better about the caliber of work my students are doing. I have a habit of imagining that other teachers all manage to get superb work out of even the most stubborn student, while I struggle on. (I have the same false concept about the way other women keep house!) I expect more of myself than is reasonable.

Not all the reflections were shallow, although many of them concentrated on editing and proofreading rather than on content. For instance, Brad wrote in his "Dear Reader" letter:

When I look at my two portfolio pieces I discover about my writing that I make very simple errors in my rough drafts. In my development of ideas, they are not very good. Also i don't like my organization of writing. It could be improved very much. I am impressed at how good my grammar and punctuation is in my writing. Sometimes I have very choppy sentences.

The comments of my peers and my teacher help me see that my writing is improving. It makes me feel really good about myself. I enjoy the response groups we have. I like for my fellow students to help me and also I like to help them.

Next time I write, I think that I will work harder on my organization. Also I want to improve my flow of ideas.

Perhaps Brad's comments had disappointed me because I knew that most of them stemmed from a grading scale form and check list that I had used to assign grades to student writing. Still, some of his observations were original. Amusingly, Brad included this letter in his final portfolio selection with this note clipped to it: "This paper is what I wrote last time when Mrs. West went to workshop."

I'm not sure what his note revealed about himself, but I sure know what it revealed about me!

After that task force session I convinced myself that I would have to allow students to choose from more than "finished" pieces of writing. From talking to Johnnie (a middle school social studies teacher in Leland, Mississippi and fellow task force member) about what she was including in her history portfolios, I discovered that my thinking had been too narrow, that if I allowed students to include "artifacts" from any area of study, including writing, descriptions of projects, test papers, vocabulary study, and so on, then the portfolio might more truly reflect that student as a writer/thinker and give the student even more autonomy over his or her portfolio selections. So, early in February I again asked students to participate in the selection and reflection process, giving them these instructions:

INSTRUCTIONS

1. Gather up all the material you have worked on this year — reading logs, journals, vocabulary, compositions, tests, projects, and other writings,

2. Choose five to ten pieces of work that match the following criteria. Remember this choice is in your judgment. Do not be unduly influenced by the grade that you may have received on that piece. Choose either draft or final copy pieces, or both.

   Criteria:

   a. Choose something that represents your typical work during each 9-weeks.

   b. Choose something that you feel is your best work.

    c. Choose something that is your favorite piece of work.

    d. Choose at least one final piece of writing.

    e. Choose two pieces which, when viewed together, will show progress you have made as a writer.

3. Decide in what order you would like to display your work, and arrange it in that order.

4. Write a paragraph to staple to the top of each piece, explaining what the assignment was, what you felt the strengths and weaknesses of your performance were, and why you chose this piece for your portfolio.

5. Write a cover letter to the people who will be reading your portfolio. Tell them what they can expect to find out about you from reading your portfolio. Tell them what you found out about yourself that you didn't know before compiling your portfolio. If you like, you can invite them to write comments back to you about what they see.

6. You may decorate your folder if you like.

Unfortunately I had not learned from my previous mistake. Again I only "took out" two days to do portfolio selection and evaluation. After all, we were right in the middle of *Macbeth*. I really did not think I could afford any more class time. But students worked diligently, and at first I was ecstatic about the results. For example, my teaching log for February 6 records:

> *Yes, yes, yes! I have just read the portfolios my students have prepared, and I am excited! They really surpassed my expectations. Overall, their comments were thoughtful and their choices judicious. I am glad that I decided to let them choose from all kinds of writing and assignments, rather than limiting the portfolio to finished pieces. The plan I started the year with is on the scrap heap. It just didn't work; this way is much better.*

Yet, at the February meeting of the task force, this time a two-day session at Lake Tiak'o khata in Louisville, Mississippi, I took a closer look at their choices. One student made no choice at all, including within his portfolio everything that had been in the "test" folder my district requires teachers to keep on each student. Many students had included a multiple choice literature test as their best work, because they had made high marks on it. That choice, in particular, bothered me. I give multiple choice tests under protest. As a Writing Project teacher, I feel that tests of this nature are not the best way to assess learning and the year before had had the freedom to test by other means. But this year the principal had indicated clearly that he expected me to give objective tests to prepare students for standardized tests they would face in other classes and in nationally normed exams. I could see his point, but still was not happy with the focus I had to give to "bubble-in" quizzes and exams. The multiple choice literature tests I gave students were a compromise, carefully crafted to give students the opportunity to practice skills of analysis, evaluation, and interpretation, and always including at least two discussion questions that required thought and expository writing skills. Even so, their inclusion as a best piece disappointed me.

Yet the students' reflections on even those choices held promise. There had been flashes of insight and an occasional perspicacious comment. Those few nuggets, perhaps, were enough to treasure. Kim even appealed to her unseen readers to add to some comments I had made about an essay she had written:

> *This is an essay question on McBeth. Mrs. West felt that I didn't have enough 'proof,' what else do you think I need?*

On another piece Kim wrote:

> *On this particular day I was thinking about what the world is coming to. This piece had many strengths because I felt strongly about what I was talking about.*

As all the task force participants gathered for the third meeting, we shared ideas and stories about what had gone on in our classrooms because of portfolios. Many, like me, were struggling with questions of choice of material and reflections on that material. I heard that day from people who were grading the whole portfolio, who were grading the individual pieces before they reached the portfolio, who were not assigning grades to any part of the portfolio. I also heard from people who limited the choices of portfolio pieces to certain kinds of work and from others who left the choice entirely up to the student. Some, like me, had changed the criteria for choosing portfolio pieces; some had not. There was a wide range of approaches and varying levels of success, but we had all come out with "enough to hold on to." And, as happens when Writing Project teachers get together, we fed from each other's successes, and helped each other think through problems.

Perhaps the most important part of the networking at this session, however, was the time we set aside to respond individually to other teachers' portfolios. We wrote notes of encouragement and support to students we had never met. Yet we felt we had met them, because in portfolio after portfolio we saw a true image of the student who had compiled it. Their "Dear Reader" letters spoke directly to us, and we spoke directly back to them. Later, when I returned to my classroom, I saw again the power of an outside audience; my students truly saw their work as important and worthwhile because of the comments my colleagues had made. One student exclaimed that she was going to put her "yellow stickies" in her senior memory book.

As we reached the closing months of a rocky year, I asked students again to choose and reflect on portfolio pieces. Again I had changed my criteria for selection. This time I told them:

INSTRUCTIONS

1. Go through your "stuff" — new and old.

2. Choose five pieces only.

    a. one "favorite"

    b. one "best"

    c. one that represents your typical work

at the beginning of the year

   d. one that represents your typical work in the middle of the year

   e. one that represents your work now

3. Guidelines:

   a. Don't include the multiple-choice part of a test. (You may include an answer to a discussion question.)

   b. You may include "stuff" from last time, but it is not essential.

   c. You can include a description of a project even if it did not produce "stuff" (oral reports, class projects), or even if you haven't yet completed it (term papers).

4. Write a cover letter for each of the five, describing briefly why you included the piece, what you liked about it, what you would change about it if you could, and what you learned from producing that piece.

5. Write a cover letter for the whole portfolio, describing what you learned from participating in the portfolio process (choosing and reflecting).

Although I glanced at the portfolios when students turned them in, in the final school rush I did not take the time to analyze them, bringing them unexamined to our last task force meeting in June. There I had time to reflect and to evaluate my experiences with the portfolio process.

I wasn't sure what I was seeing as I examined my students' final portfolios, but I definitely was seeing something. I saw that students had, while making their choices, decided on their own what was important and what wasn't, what reflected good, honest work and what didn't, how they had changed and how they had not. I saw that students had struggled to define the criteria they had used to make those judgments in clear prose evaluations addressed to specific audiences. I saw that, generally, students were proud of their growth in maturity and more confident of their abilities. Natishia's "Dear Reader" letter was the most positive:

> *From participating in the portfolio process, I was able to discover the skill of writing that I never knew I had. This whole writing process became easier and easier for me to understand. I made less errors and stuck to one subject. I became more familiar with writing in general and it doesn't take me a long time to think about what to write anymore. I feel better about my writings, and I am not scared for people to read them. I like the process. You can say it worked wonders for me. It changed my whole attitude.*

Brad's final letter was significant as well:

> *I hope that you enjoy reading my material. I have really been successful in my writings this year and have been satisfied with the topics I wrote on. It has been fun participating in the portfolio process. My writing has really improved this year a great deal.*

I also failed to find some other things I was looking for in the portfolios. I didn't find that students had an awareness of the importance of the metacognitive (or "thinking about thinking") activity in which they had engaged when writing their reflections. I missed in their end-of-the-year evaluations a sense that they had seen compiling the portfolio as a worthwhile and necessary extension of writing as a process. Still, I had not set out to find those skills in my original goals. Perhaps what I was looking for was not there because I had not asked for it. I needed another, no, several other perspectives.

My response group from the task force came to my rescue. During our June meeting at the Gulf Coast branch of the University of Southern Mississippi, task force members had all read generally through each other's portfolios over the course of several days. But I needed some specific input about what other teachers could see from my students' work. The other three people in my response group agreed to read my portfolios again and report to me on what they found.

Jane and Patsy both found evidence that students had grown and changed and, more importantly, had recognized that growth for themselves. Patsy pulled comments from cover letters and year-end evaluations that supported her point. Jane pointed out that what was not there was insignificant compared to what was there. She also showed me that in these portfolios I had physical proof of the kind of teaching that had gone on in my classroom, that I could show that the method I had used to teach had made a significant difference in students' writing abilities and maturity levels. Before her comments I had focused on what the portfolio would do for the students; now I could see what it could do for me as a teacher.

The portfolios taken as a group could give me a real indication of changes I needed to make in my teaching and in the portfolio process itself. For instance, another task force colleague noticed that the experimental nature of the portfolio process was evident in my students' comments. One of my strongest students, Paula, voiced her displeasure because we had gone back over work from the entire year each time we had selected pieces for the portfolio:

> *I feel that the portfolios are a good idea, but that we ponder on them too much. It was great at first, but now I am tired of going through it and having to look at and reanalyze the papers that we did at the beginning of the year.*

Paula's comment worried me, too, but I was not sure what method of selection would eliminate the problem, or even if the problem were widespread enough to worry about. I used other task force members as a sounding board. I wanted to discover what methods had worked for them. Both Jane and Patsy, for instance, had chosen pieces completed within a particular grading period and had not had their students reevaluate previously chosen material. Helen had asked students to choose pieces that represented a particular genre, but also pointed out to me that Paula's complaint might have been a general year-end grouse at having to work rather than a legitimate concern. Lois, too, had felt that Paula's comment might have been an isolated belly-ache, soon cured with an aspirin and a vacation. Yet I had felt the boredom hanging in the air over that last selection process, and I was not sure that I could write it off to "senior-itis."

Finally, my venture into the portfolio process had harvested a profitable catch: my nets were full. First, my students had gained autonomy, had analyzed their growth in writing and thinking over time, and had shown pride in their work. Second, I had proof of a successful year of teaching students to think for themselves, whether they wanted to or not. Third, I had evidence that I could use to reexamine my teaching methods, so that I could use evaluation as a basis for improvement. Fourth, I had had a chance to analyze, evaluate, discuss, compare, improve, argue, think, and make decisions about students' work and about my teaching, a process that, whatever the outcome, can only result in improvement of teaching and learning. I didn't find everything I had set out to find, but I discovered lots of information that was significant. Of course, anytime you haul in a fishing net, or a portfolio, you are going to get lots of unidentifiable wiggly sea creatures that you didn't expect to find. And sometimes those strange and curious creatures, upon closer examination, are just as valuable as what you set out to catch.

A First Grade Perspective

Lois R. Brandts

A California teacher invites parents into the portfolio process she uses with first graders. That process spans the entire year, during which students learn the confidence and craft necessary to assemble and to reflect on showcase portfolios.

The portfolio is more than the work it contains; its strength lies in the process of how it is used. Portfolios become evidence of growth and change over time in terms of reflection, involvement in long-term projects, self-concept, and visual awareness.
— Robert J. Tierney

Four children sat huddled on the carpet in a first grade classroom in late May. On the floor in front of each was a stack of papers. Attending to his own accumulation of work, each child began to sort through the stack. One began by picking up a paper, gazing at it intently, and mouthing the words on the page. Occasionally she leaned over to ask another child, "What does this say?" Together they figured it out or abandoned it to start decoding a new piece. One boy burst into laughter saying, "Can you believe this, Mrs. Brandts? I can't even read what I wrote. Oh, no." Then he marched proudly around the room showing anyone interested just what he had not been able to do earlier in the year. The implication was that he had progressed so far from his original attempts that he now could confidently invite others to share in his

107

derision of himself and his earlier efforts. Not only could he write, but he could also read what he wrote. He was now a writer. He was now a member of the club (Smith, 1988).

> *Look at me, I am a pirate. I have a big sword. I fight other pirates. They might kill me but I kill them. I climb down steps. My name is Ken. I am the best pirate. I like to dream and sometimes dreams come true.* Tell Payne (7 years)

Around the room other groups of four were going through the same process with similar reactions. Gradually, as quiet hushed tones gave way to their normal buoyant voices, more children began to move about, sharing a piece of writing first with one friend and then another. There was an air of excitement in the room and, within minutes, a full-fledged first grade version of a noisy "publishing party" was under way. I brought out the cider and cookies and we punctuated our celebration with a toast to ourselves and one another.

Situated in a school of 582 children in Goleta, California, this first grade consisted of twenty-eight children, five of whom were bilingual. Eight of the children were sent to the reading specialist for a daily half hour of instruction, two went out for speech and language instruction twice a week, five saw the English Second Language teacher three times each week, and two saw the school counselor on a regular basis. There was some overlapping, that is, some children were pulled out more than once. Four mothers volunteered an hour a week to help in the classroom and there was an aide for two and one-half hours Monday through Thursday. Approximately half of the children came from families where both parents worked outside the home, generally in service-oriented jobs. Seven of the children were from single-parent homes and two from dual custody arrangements.

Overall, the class was wildly exuberant and often volatile. The yard duty personnel and other teachers frequently had to intervene in confrontations. Several of the boys worked at the art of rug-rolling, practicing it with determined persistence. During nondirected instructional time the noise level often became unacceptable, prompting a substitute teacher to leave me a note asking if I had changed the class rules from "Speak in a soft voice" to "Yell whenever you get the chance."

Not visible on first appearance was how the culture of the classroom had evolved to bring the children to an understanding of themselves as participants in their own learning. From the first day of school, I incorporated community-building activities and daily writing time. In September I sent each child a personalized letter at home welcoming them to school, and I invited each child and parent to join the community of first grade readers and writers. I also invited them to bring a favorite book for me to read during the first few getting-acquainted days. I put copies of my letter and a notation of the title of the book they brought into each child's writing folder. If a child did not bring a book I made a note of that; in this way I began my own assessment of the home support provided for each child.

During the first week of school I gave parents a homework assignment titled "Love Letter," which said, "I want to fall in love with your child. You have had several years to get to know one another intimately but I only have a few months to be with your child. Tell me all of the wonderful things about your child. You can brag to your heart's content ..." (Calkins, 1990). And brag they did. The letters usually contained detailed contents about the child's life, and the language was warm and authentic.

I assured parents that letters would be returned in the child's portfolio at the end of the year. All work remained in the classroom for the child to look at. Nothing brightened up children's faces so much as sitting down with me as I quietly read them their special letter.

Introducing writing workshop at the beginning of the third week was easy enough when the children saw that there were already artifacts in their folder, one from their teacher and one from a parent. The sense of adding a piece of their own seemed comfortable and natural. Initially, the emerging writers feared attempting anything that might be "wrong," but with time began to understand that putting down the sounds they heard was "right." Gradually, they began to take some risks as they strove for fluency. Writing was beginning to be fun, and we were building a community of trust. The proof came sometime in late November when I was out ill for several days. Upon my return to the classroom one child called out, "We didn't like it when you were gone. We didn't do writing workshop *once!*" Students did not miss me as much as this essential part of the program that they had come to view as their own. On my first day back, Stephanie wrote this. It was one of the selections that she picked to include in her finished portfolio several months later.

Stephanie

my Little Sister

whin my Little Sister

was baorn I was iksidid

uhin my mom came home

my Sisters Birth day

is on Lanuwf[ærry

14th

In mid-October, after we had been in school a little over a month, I sent a notice home requesting that parents sign up for a home visit. The response was overwhelming. In all but a few instances, children and parents welcomed me to their homes and apartments, where they shared cookies, tea, cokes, their bedroom, their collections, and above all, their manners. I carried their writing folders with me, more to give the parents a quick glimpse of progress than anything else. When I left each home, I felt I knew each child more intimately. Because we had made a personal connection, together we were able to put at least half a dozen new topics in folders under "Things to Write About." The reward for me outweighed the time I gave up visiting the homes. For those children whose parents did not sign up for a visit, I provided a space for "Home to School," so they could bring a collection of interests to share and discuss with me and the other children.

Parents Are Part of the Process

During the year I continued to invite parents into the process. At first, I advised them that no written stories would be coming home but that I would save them at school. I assured them that they were welcome to come by at any time and browse through their child's folder to see what progress was taking place. The children had easy access to the hanging folders where we stored the writing and often demanded, "Look at what I wrote!" when a parent came to pick them up. Their pride and ownership did more to convince the parents of the value of our program than any of my informational letters. The writing folders became the main focus of discussion at the first parent conference in November.

Three times during the year I asked the children to spread out everything that was in their folder to see if there were some pieces of writing that they valued over others. Each child then met privately in conference with me or a teaching aide and picked out his or her three best pieces. I told the children that I also got to pick a piece each time. I asked questions that encouraged beginning writers to reflect on their reasons for selection. In the first part of the year, an adult helper wrote down the child's reflection at the end of the story.

When My Cat Had Kittens

*We went to the beach and when we got back our cat was
getting ready to have kittens. The first one that came was
black. The last one died. It was so beautiful. I wish she never
died. The end.* (Alisha Adams, 7 years)

Alisha's reflection was short, to the point, and appropriate for
a first grader. She said, "I like my story about birthdays because
I like cats." Often I worried about the brevity of some of their
responses. Once, in my research group, I described my concern
that children write longer reflective pieces. One of my colleagues
thought a moment and then said, "Should we realistically expect
six feet of growth when they have only lived three?" She was
surprised at her own response and began to laugh. Because we all
knew that it was true, we collapsed into laughter and practiced
our adult version of rug-rolling, sharing a moment of hilarity and
truth.

In the winter I provided another time for selecting, reflecting,
and transferring work from the folder into the permanent portfolio, but this time the children were able to do the task more easily
on their own. Some began to question whether it might be
acceptable to take out something they had put in the portfolio
earlier and put in more recent writing that they considered to be
better. When I told them that they were free to make switches
based upon more recent work, some of them lost little time
including samples that they believed to be better writing.

In the spring we decorated our Showcase Portfolios, a culmi-
nation of the best selections that the child, parent, and teacher had
made of the child's year as a writer. I used expandable folders as
my portfolios because many of the projects and products that the
first graders created and chose didn't fit into a neat eight-and-a-
half by eleven format.

Again, I met with each child, but by now I was more a
spectator in the process. One little girl spent several minutes
telling me how she felt about her work. She had been shy when
she entered first grade, reluctant to write at all. Now, eight months
later, she saw herself as a writer, and was eager to share every-

thing she was going to include in her final selection with me. She agreed to read several pieces aloud and for the camera that I had set up if I agreed to help her with any words with which she might have a problem. Her only difficulty in making her selections was that she had many pieces that she really liked. When I asked her what it was that she liked about them, she said, "I like them because they are *long!*" Tanya concluded that she had no choice but to pick several more pieces of work, and was in the process of doing that, so I thanked her and moved away to help another child. The camera, however, was still trained on Tanya. That night, as I viewed the film, I was deeply touched by what I saw. As she gathered up her papers, Tanya had paused and said to no one in particular, "Now, *that* was a conference."

Wn   I   Late

at   The

Octaps   The   Octaps

Is   Sac

Aot   and

Tan   We   Latc

At   The   Raes   The

Rae   Was   a   Mata Rae

The scene described in the opening paragraphs of this article did not happen without a great deal of work and preparation. By the time I asked the children to sit together at the end of the school year, select best pieces, reflect on their choices, and then move them from folder to showcase portfolio, these children were confident in their craft. They had little problem determining what made a piece of writing worth keeping and what set a written piece apart from many of the others. As I watched Alisha, Tanya, Stephanie, and Tell pour over their work, I realized the great value of keeping portfolios for children in the early primary grades. But I discovered that it had to be a process over time, a process for the children, for the parents, and especially for me, the teacher. Any attempt to shortcut would make portfolio results less successful.

One of the last tasks of the year was another exchange of letter writing. I asked each child to write a letter, "To the Reader of My Portfolio." I asked them to discuss in it why they picked the pieces they did, what those pieces told about them as writers, and how they felt about writing. Beforehand, I discussed who their audience might be: teacher, family, neighbors, friends, next year's teacher.

To the Reader of My Portfolio

I picked the Day of My Birthday because I liked what I wrote. I picked I went to the L.A. zoo because I had a fun time. I picked when my friends spended the night because I like to play with my friends. I picked my journal because it was one of my first things that I worked with. I think that writing is fun. I think that I write much better.

We modeled how to present a portfolio to someone to read, and I encouraged each child to make an appointment with next year's teacher to share the contents. Each child then took his or her portfolio home to share with parents and family. I made a homework request for each member of the family to look it over carefully and then to write a letter to the child about it. Those letters were powerful affirmations of the connection between parents and child based on the child's writing.

May 7. 1992

Dear Alisha,
    I just read your work
from your writing portfolio.
I really enjoyed your stories!
    Your spelling has really
improved since the first day of
first grade. So has your handwriting.
    I found out more about
you by reading your stories and
I always like finding out more
about you!
    I look forward to reading
more of your stories in the
future. Keep up the good work,
you are a great author.

           I Love You,
              Mom
P.S. I liked the story about Cally's
babies and about Jessie and Lacey.

Letter from Alisha's mother

Lastly, I wrote a personal letter thanking each child for his or her hard work and to the parents for their support and cooperation.

Three years ago when I first began using portfolios, I already had writing workshop firmly in place. I had been a Fellow in the South Coast Writing Project since 1984 and had participated in the Literature Institute and Advanced Literature Institute since 1988. I had spent several years working out structure and management strategies for teaching first graders. Each year I had sent home a large pile of writing for each child, along with some published books, thinking to myself, "So what?" Portfolios came along at a time to match the questions I was beginning to have. I was unsure of the unknowns. How was I going to manage all of this? Who wanted to know and why? Was this just another fly-by-night idea that would soon pass?

After careful consideration, I decided to attempt portfolio-keeping with only six out of the twenty-eight children in our class. It was a difficult but wise decision. I felt some degree of guilt and worried over the ones not selected. I was careful to choose a range of children and abilities that represented the overall makeup of the class. In that way I was able to work out most of the difficult management and logistic problems that sometimes doom a good idea to failure. Because I did take that time, I then knew where I was going and why.

Portfolios as Idea-Exchange

When the concept of using portfolios as a tool to assess children's academic growth first appeared, the idea excited and challenged teachers. Some had been participants in Writing Projects and were current with the latest ideas from reading professional publications. Teachers began to ally themselves with teacher researcher groups, as I did, where there was idea-exchange advice on better teaching practices. My first attempts were slow and uneven as I worked my way through the process. I felt that portfolio assessment was too good an idea to misunderstand, misinterpret, or misuse. My teammates and administrator gave me their support and that added to my willingness to take the necessary risks.

Throughout the state of California and across the nation, portfolio inservices have been presented to overflow audiences. The same wild enthusiasm that sparked the rush to technology has characterized the headlong plunge into the use of portfolios in classrooms, schools, and districts. At national conferences the word "portfolio" in the title assures the presenter of a large and attentive audience. As educators with good intentions march in and out of these sessions, it is difficult to judge how effectively practices are being used in classrooms across the country. Now that the idea of authentic assessment has circulated widely and the word "portfolio" has ceased to be a buzzword, can we stand back and ask ourselves, "What's working and what's not? Can we fix it if it isn't working?" I keep asking myself, "What would cause it to fail?" I now think I know.

I do not want portfolios to become an academic mantra, with the implication that by their use teachers will somehow finally find the one right answer to the question of assessment. It is essential for educators to step back and take a look at the big picture, and, in some localities, at the implications of a changing student population. Teachers themselves need to assess the uses and meaning that portfolios may have in the lives of the children whom they teach. For me, portfolios provide a strong link between home and school, and they help me involve parents in recognizing and respecting their child's growth. I believe that portfolio use can be invaluable if teachers are given the time to reflect, refine, and select what is comfortable and meaningful for them. They need time to answer the question, "Who wants to know and why?" Above all, they need time to put classroom teaching practices in place that allow children choice, structure, response, and community. Often, teachers who come to learn about portfolio use discover that they need to back up and introduce writing techniques before they can begin to implement portfolios. Growth and change take patience and time. Portfolios as a means of authentic assessment will only be as successful as the good teaching practices that are in place with them.

References

Calkins, L. (1990). *Living between the lines*. Portsmouth, NH: Heinemann.

Smith, F. (1988). *Joining the literacy club: Further essays into education*. Portsmouth, NH: Heinemann.

Tierney, R., Carter, M., & Desai, L. (1991). *Portfolio assessment in the reading-writing classroom*. Norwood, MA: Christopher-Gordon.

Listening to Gia

Susan Reed

A California teacher emphasizes constant revising, responding, and reflecting in her urban portfolio classroom. She demonstrates through the processes of one student how this kind of classroom can engage and influence both students and teacher.

In Chapter One of *Portfolio Portraits,* Donald Graves urges teachers to avoid closing down on the notion of what the portfolio can do in the classroom. He wants us to keep a good idea growing by asking teachers and students to get involved in what the portfolio can look like and how it can be a learning tool for both student and teacher. He says:

> *Students are used to being told what is good and not good in their work. If students are to improve their own judgment about their work, and if their work is to show improvement because of their own struggle with quality, a different use of class and teacher time is required. From the outset, students must be helped to make judgments about their work. Rather than quickly assembling work in May for the annual portfolio review, students must constantly shuffle their work and write letters and other statements in which they evaluate their work throughout the year. This is slow work for both teacher and student. (3)*

In my urban school classes we now make a different use of class and teacher time; we do the Graves' shuffle all year long. Work on portfolios must begin way before portfolios are actually due. In September, thinking I'm the one who does the shuffling, my students are usually ready to give over every scrap of their writing to me. "You want these?" is the question of the month. Even after I say, "No, hold on to them," I still find two or three in my In Box at the end of each class. Portfolio work means learning how to use the teacher in different ways. And portfolio work means staying open, taking risks, and thinking a lot before closing down on ideas.

More specifically, in my El Cerrito, California, classroom, portfolio work means reflecting regularly in journals, selecting and revising several journal entries, writing in a variety of genres, collecting pieces together in packets from which to reflect more about the processes of reading and writing. The packets become the products for the portfolios; the constant revising, responding, and reflecting are the essence of the portfolios.

For example, a portfolio classroom, as I see it, starts with the journal entries my students write. When we read Steinbeck's *Of Mice and Men*, they write to specific prompts that encourage them to get inside the skins of the characters: interior monologues for Crooks and Curley's wife or unwritten dialogues between Curley and his wife. They write about dreams — in the novel as well as in their own lives. They consider abstract ideas like loyalty and friendship. Each time they write, they read their work to a partner, and we use the writing to fire our class discussions.

They also write their own reflections and questions (we call them "thinkwrites" or reading log entries) on the novel as well as a variety of short readings we all bring to class: an article on California migrant workers by Cesar Chavez; newspaper accounts of the homeless; Steinbeck's letter to an actress preparing for the role of Curley's wife; interviews by Studs Terkel on living through the depression (from *Hard Times*) and on the dreams we hold for ourselves (*American Dreams: Lost and Found*).

Each student writes ten or twelve such entries before I ask her to review all of what she has written, and to revise just one entry

— one of her choosing. This task is tough to do at first since the idea of choice is hard. "How do I know what's best?" she asks. "How do I know what I like? I mean, what are we *supposed* to like?" Too few students know what's good until they see a teacher's grade on their work. "I don't know what you want," she says to me. I need to help her figure out for herself what she's got; it's hard for any of us to take stock of ourselves alone. Her classmates help her do that. She works with three other students at her table. After a few weeks, she starts to say, "The help [from classmates] I got on this writing was good ... I got to see what the reader wanted to know, not just what I first thought I had to say." In class, she hears a lot of student writing read aloud at her table as well as to the whole class. She begins to understand that making choices from her log is part of the portfolio process.

We also pause regularly, usually when we finish reading a book or at the end of a month, and do some more choosing and rewriting. Each student puts together a packet of writing that includes reading logs, revisions of log entries, several drafts of a chosen piece of writing that started earlier, and written peer responses to those drafts. I ask that they complete The Last Word, a page of questions about the process I have just described, and attach it to the top of the packet. My students practice this kind of thinking and writing all through the year, whether or not they actually choose to put these pieces of writing in their portfolios at the end of the term. Through this process they get used to thinking about choices and changes; they become more independent and self-reliant.

As a way of illustrating what I mean, I would like to ask you to listen to one of my tenth-grade students, as she reflects on the work she's done on *Of Mice and Men*. My first question on The Last Word is:

> *Please explain your writing process for this piece. Where did the idea start, how did it change, what did you see happening to your writing? Provide a context for your readers to better understand your writing.*

Here is Gia's answer:

My writing process for this piece of writing is quite a nightmare. At first, I was thinking that I'd do an interior monologue of how George felt about Lennie. It seemed great to me that showing George's secret loathing of Lennie would be fun but then it seemed too dull and unexciting.

So I thought of tackling Lennie's mind since it was much harder to understand and did start off my writing having Lennie say the things that go on in his mind. In my 1st draft, I gathered in most of what Lennie says or thought about a lot and made it into a really short and quick monologue.

When my table heard it, they said it was good but my writing was just like copying things out of the book and not original enough. This thought hit me hard so what I did next was rewrite the first draft and made the second draft completely different. What I mean is I did have Lennie doing an interior monologue but this piece of writing was showing a different side of Lennie, an intelligence of him which was supposed to show his innocence and confusion. It was written too unrealistically after I thought about it for awhile, so I left that idea and tackled the most difficult meaning of the book to me, which was the deep love George felt for Lennie that made him kill him in the end.

By now, I was desperate and really unsure of myself because each of my 2 prior drafts were totally different and I wasn't sure how I'd handle this 3rd one. Without thinking, I just slowly "freewrote" for a while and I soon gathered up my thoughts and strung them all together to form a poem. I couldn't believe what I did because not only did it make sense but I understood George's love for Lennie from reading what I wrote. It was scary but I knew that this final poem was what I really wanted to work on.

Gia is proud of her poem but she also can be proud that she knows for herself how far she has come with her work.

Right from the beginning she thinks about the form her writing will take: the monologues. In fact, the idea of the form she can use seems to drive her on from one draft to the next. The monologues serve her as a way into the characters' minds — how George felt about Lennie; what Lennie is thinking; how Lennie is really innocent and confused.

Gia also offers a fine testimonial to the use of writing to discover what she thinks; she understands the power of writing to help her learn. All the way through her packet of work about *Of Mice and Men*, from her log entries to her poem, Gia examines and questions this troublesome relationship between Lennie and George. And later, in readying herself to try a third draft of her work, she says she tried a "freewrite" and found another way to look at this issue: through the voice of her poem. It is her own poem that helps her understand what she has been struggling with all through the novel, and she knows it.

Gia listens to her classmates' response to her work, even when it isn't very encouraging. ("They said it was good but my writing was just like copying things out of the book and not original enough.") She values what they say and uses it to help her go forth with something entirely different: "This thought hit me hard so what I did next was rewrite the first draft and made the second draft completely different."

Testing Theories

It's clear Gia has some working theories about what helps her write, and she knows she can try them again for the next piece of writing. This is what happens in a portfolio classroom where we test our theories and act on our experience. For instance, she recognizes that staying flexible and trying variety can help. There is no one easy path to follow from the start of an idea to a finished piece of writing. No formula. She knows she can call upon several resources to help her when she's stuck: response groups, freewriting, and time. She recognizes that perseverance pays off. She's come up with a theory, one I hope she'll test again and again, that if she heads straight for the most troubling, frustrating part of her reading she can make sense of it through her own writing.

A portfolio classroom invites both of us to learn. As her teacher, I also can learn from Gia's answer; it has implications for my teaching. For instance, I learn that writing response groups can be helpful in unpredictable ways. The kind of help her group offered her, the help that pushed her forward to re-see her own work, is not the kind of help I usually encourage as her teacher. I can hear myself admonishing the group: "Where could she add detail? *Where* are you confused? Please don't just tell her it's 'uninteresting.' Tell her what you would like to hear more about!" Yet, I can see what she did. Unlike many of my students who would have tinkered with a few words of their first drafts or added whatever details their response partners specifically requested, Gia drastically changes her own work, beginning anew with the next draft.

So Gia's story encourages me to question my thinking about response groups and how they work. Her story tells me to allow for ways to leave the door open for the unexpected to happen, to trust that talk about writing can yield surprising results.

What jumps out at me as I learn from Gia's story is that she remains undaunted in the face of her difficulties. She uses words like "nightmare," "desperate," and "scary" to describe this process. She loses her footing along the way to her poem and yet she keeps going. Why? To make sense of what she didn't understand? To transform her work from something "dull and unexciting" to something "original"? To find something she "really wanted to work on"?

When I listen to her account of her own work, I recognize how hard she works. What a context I have for the final draft she submitted: a twenty-line poem!

Stories like Gia's help me bring genuine questions to all the student packets. For instance, how many of my students really take the risks Gia does? And if they do, how many of them panic when they "lose control" of writing the way she does? When writing changes as the letters unfurl before their eyes, do they become uneasy? Do they stop writing? Or does that uneasiness spur them on?

Questions Drive More Questions

These questions and many others like them drive me back into my classroom to talk to my students, to watch them at work, to ask them more questions. I want to learn more of how they work in writing groups, of how they move from one idea to the next, of gathering up their thoughts to "string them all together," as Gia puts it, from draft to draft of their writing.

By the end of the term, Gia will have an extraordinary collection of journal entries, reading log entries, drafts, and polished pieces of writing she chose to write as she read *Of Mice and Men*, *Macbeth*, *Cry, the Beloved Country*, and *Black Boy*, as well as an assortment of self-selected readings by predominantly African-American writers. She also will have done a considerable amount of thinking about her own writing in several journal entries as well as about the Last Words of packets. When she chooses among these pieces to represent her in her portfolio, she provides herself, her family, the school, and the outside world with information that differs greatly from the collection of test scores and grades in her school folder. When she describes and judges her own work, she learns she doesn't need to sit back and wait for somebody else to tell her how she is doing or what to try next. Nor do I. We are learning to see ourselves through our work.

Reference

Graves, D., & Sunstein, B. (1992). *Portfolio portraits*. Portsmouth, NH: Heinemann.

Interviewing Students About Their Portfolios

Bob Ingalls and Joyce Jones

Two Virginia teachers discover through their department's teacher research project the value of having students narrate their portfolios. They discuss the nature of this narration and how it adds a needed dimension to portfolio assessment of writing.

In January, 1985, the English department at Mount Vernon High School voluntarily began to assess the quality of student writing in writing portfolios. Today we continue to assess our students' portfolios, but the procedure is much different than the one we used initially. After unsuccessfully struggling to evaluate portfolios in the same way we evaluated single writing assignments — reading them without the writer present — we learned the limits to such evaluation and discovered the differences between portfolios and single writings.

For years our department had required teachers to maintain student folders that included anything related to writing, spelling worksheets included, and to pass these folders on to the next teacher at the end of each year. We started in 1985 by talking about portfolio standards and ways to improve these messy cumulative folders. The first step was to set portfolio requirements. Our goal was not to change curriculum or teaching practices. Rather, our goal was to study student writing, so we decided to simply set a maximum number of pieces and to ask for a variety of writing. We required that students, not teachers, be responsible for completing a table of contents, keeping rough drafts, writing a reflective piece about the portfolio, and separating writings by years.

Nine months later, in September, 1985, we randomly selected a group of thirty freshmen to follow for four years, planning to evaluate their portfolios each year. Throughout that year English teachers prepared for the assessment by reading whatever had been written about portfolios (very little in 1985), and the department brainstormed and discussed various ways to use portfolios in the classroom. Though we said evaluating portfolios would be different from scoring single writing assignments, we unconsciously limited ourselves to what we knew about evaluating writing. By January we had developed portfolio judging criteria (We called it our portfolio rubric because it resembled what we used for grading writing tests.) It included instruction on such things as writing unity, things that explained the quality of a well-written essay but that confused us when applied to a portfolio. We agreed to begin in June, after students were gone — an appropriate time for evaluation, we felt.

In the beginning ...

Our portfolio assessments were quite conventional. Fourteen of us gathered together to score the sample group of thirty cumulative portfolios. The first year represented the work from the freshman English classes. We followed these students for four years.

Linda Durrell arrives early on the teacher work day. She sees the thirty targeted student portfolios stacked on the table and multiple copies of the rubric the department has developed to evaluate them.Once the other teachers arrive, Ms. Durrell and her fellow English teachers discuss the rubric, clarifying terms like "completeness." Ms. Durrell asks about "revision" and how she is to judge it. There is some uncertainty, but the department agrees to look at the rough drafts for evidence of revision and to read the students' reflection letters for clues.

Linda Durrell joins Marge Evans to discuss their observations of one of the cumulative portfolios. Fifteen minutes later they talk with the rest of the department about the rubric. Ms. Durrell asks why the portfolios don't have rough drafts. When Bill Gage says many of his students revise on word processors and don't always save their earlier drafts, Ms. Durrell senses the complexity of portfolio assessment.

Ms.Durrell and her partner read another portfolio and score it according to the department rubric. She wants to know why there was so little revision in the "letter to a favorite author" assignment.

Two hours later, Ms. Durrell and Ms. Evans have scored five portfolios. During the post-scoring discussion Ms. Durrell asks her revision question. Jim Crown explains his letter assignment; and other teachers respond by explaining similar assignments. The discussion ends with Ms. Durrell still wondering.

For four years we were dissatisfied with our assessment results; we scored thirty portfolios, but there was little exhilaration in the postscoring discussion. It produced more criticism than understanding of student writing. To improve the process, after the second year we made our scoring guide more general, encouraging more comments than numbers. Then we set clearer department standards for portfolios to improve their readability. Finally, to decrease defensiveness, we interviewed teachers of the sample students when their student portfolios were being evaluated.

Our greatest difficulty was understanding the context for the writing. What was assigned? Who read it? What resources were available or used? What did the teacher say? We tried to see where the student writer fit into the writing class and to understand the role of the teacher. Did Kendra choose the excellent images in her poem, or did the teacher lead her to this discovery? When the portfolio was sloppy or lacking in quality writing, had the teacher not guided students in preparing their portfolios or did the students have poor writing or organization skills? These questions only created more questions, for when we began dissecting Kendra's process, we needed more information than the portfolio provided. Without the student writer present, we had to recreate the context, not just for one writing but for many, each with its unique circumstances. We wanted the portfolios to explain or demonstrate what was happening in our writing classrooms. Rather than answering questions, they raised more:

Why was so little revision evident in the portfolios?

Why was there so little evidence of beautiful or powerful language?

Why were the writings so error free?

Why was there so little evidence of self-selected topics?

There were clues in every portfolio, but nothing conclusive. When the scoring ended, we teachers hadn't discovered much. Familiar judgments became answers:

Students are too lazy to revise.

Students don't read enough.

Teachers have to do too much of the correcting.

Students do better when they are assigned a topic.

In time ...

We discovered the value of interviewing our sample group of students about their portfolios. When we extended the community, or actually included everyone who really belonged in the writing community (both teachers and students), something changed profoundly.

Richard is one of thirty students invited in the middle of the school day to discuss his portfolio. He is a high school senior and has been part of a four-year assessment study of Mount Vernon High School's writing program. Each year he has returned to review his writings and explain to teachers and students his views on writing assignments and instruction at his high school.

Ms. Durrell and other teachers greet Richard and the other students and assist them in reviewing and discussing their portfolios. In his small group Richard talks about his frustrations with essay assignments, "especially when a certain topic is required." Then he listens to Kendra talk of her love for her ninth grade poetry and Allison's surprise at how much she wrote in eleventh grade. At the end Richard agrees to be the spokesperson and report their findings to the large group.

In the large group students and teachers listen to Richard's report, comparing what he says to what the other groups have said. After nearly two hours, the group of teachers and students reaches several conclusions about writing at the school, conclusions based on portfolio evidence and explanations from student writers. The evidence and conclusions become the data for multiple teacher discussions to take place over the next few months.

Students used their experiences as writers and researchers to examine and analyze their portfolios before participating in discussion. They spoke with assurance, sincerity, and honesty. They believed what they were saying, and they believed that we were truly interested. Their responses were based not only on feelings, but also on discoveries they had made in their portfolio work. Their responses could be measured against the responses of other students experiencing the same research and evaluation. They could validate their findings or have them challenged by fellow writers. And instead of teachers telling them what it all meant, Ms. Durrell and other teachers were asking them what they thought it all meant. When they responded, teachers took notes, asked questions, asked for clarification, speculated on the significance of student findings — in short, valued them and their writing experiences. There was a community. The evaluators now included teachers as well as students who understood what they had done in their portfolios. Together they worked to find additional meaning in their portfolios.

Of particular interest is the effect these portfolio interviews had on teachers. When we looked at how these student-teacher discussions affected individual teachers, we had to stop and ask: What happened here? What does it mean? For years teachers had assessed student portfolios, only to restate their same convictions and judgments. After meeting with students and listening to them talk about writing, teachers began to hear in a new way. Students told us how grading affected their writing processes:

> Allison: (after examining her portfolio) *When I write to a friend and I know it's not being graded, I express myself more, but when I know it's being graded, I don't experiment.*

131

Kendra: *I think when a teacher is reading the stories … they don't really think about how much effort you put into it … they grade it on spelling and paragraphs, not on whether you took the time to come up with your own thoughts and write them down on paper … Writing standard things is easier to get higher grades.*

Richard: *When I write something right the first time, and I get graded down because I don't have several drafts, I don't like it when the teacher requires a certain number of drafts.*

This gave us insight into our role as teachers …

Mr. Gage: (during the interview) *I was surprised what a negative factor grading is. The rejection and criticism hurts them … from what they were saying grading gets in the way of their honesty. They end up writing just to do what the teacher wants. And I don't like having to grade either. I wish I didn't have to do it.*

Unlike the teacher evaluation sessions, the portfolio-interview assessment encouraged understanding. But why? How?

First, the portfolios helped the students be more reflective and objective.

Roy: *I don't have much variety. I should experiment with it and try different styles of writing.*

Anna: *I got out of the habit of writing stories, and I'm finding it hard to pick that back up this year with all the essays and papers we write now.*

Second, sitting with students who were going through this process helped teachers see beyond their last assignment.

Mr. Gage: *… the point of what was said … not all writing needs to be revised. Sometimes we give them a choice of topics, other times we give* *them complete freedom. But the variety the students want more of seems related to the amount of revision as well as the forms. They may want to leave it as it is.*

Ms. Durrell: *Requiring feedback on every writing is like mandating all students to write three drafts or five paragraphs for an essay. Everyone's process is different.*

Teacher-student interaction gave a fuller vision of student writing, something we were only able to achieve when we included students in the discussion of writing instruction. There was a balance of positive and negative points, with the final student-teacher discussion resembling a community celebration of the writing of students and the teaching of the department.

Allison: *Over the past four years we (the group of students) have been able to see, unlike our other classes, what we have learned. I can look back at my papers and see how I can change them. Four years ago I couldn't have done that. We could see how English will help us ... like later on.*

Richard: *We said that over the last four years we have written almost everything. We said we could go into college and not be frightened when teachers said to do something and we wouldn't know how to write it. We've written short stories, essays, research papers ...*

Kendra: *And when I see my folder, I'm surprised I wrote all this kind of stuff. Like wow, you know?*

Gary: *I never really think about what I have learned in math ... I mean, you just do problems ... but as you look back on this (portfolio), you see actual progress ... you'd never think you would.*

Teachers liked what they heard:

Mr. Gage: *I found it very interesting that they are able to see improvement in English. I find that rather odd because initially people would see English as all the same ... but when they took a look at their papers, they could see improvement they couldn't see in their other subjects. I thought it was great.*

Portfolios provide wonderful data for writing teachers to study. However, only when the student writers themselves are part of the study can teachers truly understand what the data is showing them. Portfolios become more valuable when kept in the hands of the writers. Separating them from the writers complicates the assessment task, may confuse the evaluators, and rarely provides insights into the writing program. We are finding that the portfolio interview process is a model of learning that both students and teachers can use to better understand writing process, writing growth, and writing programs. This evaluation encourages teachers to include students in decision-making and to lead students in evaluating their own writing.

As with any experimental model, our student interview process was not without problems. Having students released from other classes, tape-recording and transcribing student-teacher discussions, and finding time to analyze data all proved to be challenging tasks. Sometimes we had to go to classrooms to explain personally to other teachers why we really needed Roy or Kendra to join us in our interviews. Videotaping could be the solution to the tedious task of transcribing tape recordings. Getting administrative support in the form of substitutes so that teachers can work together to analyze data is a must.

In every English class we are presently using a streamlined portfolio interview that is less time-consuming and more workable. Teachers and students use the portfolios as the starting place to discuss how writing is taught and learned, and to set goals for future writing instruction. On Portfolio Pick-Up Day students return to last year's English teacher to retrieve their writing portfolios. After ten minutes they return to this year's English class and quietly read through their folders, reflecting on what they like, what is missing, and what they need to work on. After this personal reflection, students gather in small groups to discuss what they have noticed in the portfolios. Finally, the teacher leads a whole class discussion of what the portfolios reveal and where the class needs to go with writing this year.

We believe the portfolio is a better tool for assessment than it is a target in itself. When Richard used the tool to understand himself and we listened, together we became a learning community.

> Richard: *Looking at my portfolio during the interview has helped me. Being able to look over my stories and see how I grew as a writer ... and what I've learned. There's a lot of things you learn in English that you can't really see.*

Vermont Writing Portfolios

Fern Tavalin

A Vermont teacher and her students participate in the first statewide portfolio assessment. She notes the advantages and drawbacks of this assessment as well as how it works with her established classroom practices.

I am an eighth grade English teacher in the state of Vermont. Like hundreds of Vermont teachers, I was told that a writing portfolio assessment would be mandatory beginning in the spring of 1992. The following is my account of the first year.

Because my students have always maintained writing folders and receive frequent essay assignments in social studies, science, art, and health, the portfolio requirement seemed like a request to collect what was already being done — a matter that should have taken an afternoon of organizing. However, through the experience of assembling student writings, I have come to understand certain characteristics of performance assessment and the value students give to their work that make this process more complex than I originally thought.

My writing classes alternate between direct grammar instruction and critique sessions. The writing critique groups each comprise twelve students who gather while the rest of the class works independently. Students select pieces they would like to bring before their group and distribute copies for peer comment prior to the critique session. Each writing goes through at least two types of review. First, a piece is read for enjoyment, appreciation, and questioning. We work in a circle where everyone participates in turn. I act as a scribe for student comments, as well as make contributions of my own. Students begin by describing what they see in a particular writing. They make comments such as "not mentioning the sex of the main character really gives my mind a chance to imagine different things" or, "when you call it a black rose it creates suspense for me because I sense beauty and danger." Students note techniques or stylistic traits of the author and frequently mention the feelings evoked by the writing. When the group has finished describing the author's work, students ask questions that emerge from the piece. "Why did you decide to leave such an open ending?" "What does the main character look like?" "Is this happening in the present or the past?" Often these questions lead to clarification and further elaboration in subsequent drafts. As one student put it, "We come to class determined to show our peers our abilities, our writing, which can be considered as a part of our hearts and our minds."

Personalized Lessons

Once an author brings a piece to what he or she believes is a final draft, the group reads and comments on mechanics. I begin by asking if anyone has noticed a pattern to the mechanical errors. Then, we look specifically for that type of error. This provides a focus and a personalized lesson from which many in the group can benefit. The nature of the mechanics review can vary from mundane spelling searches to intensely thought-provoking discussions about style. For example, the author of one piece commented that she had deliberately included fragments to give the feeling of rapid thoughts and actions. The group then identified all the fragments and reread the piece aloud to discuss which fragments served the author's intent and which ones distracted the reader. The author commented about one sentence that met with mixed reviews, "Well, I guess this call is up to me."

The questions my students ask each other fit quite naturally into the five dimensions the State of Vermont has established to score student portfolios: purpose, organization, details, voice/tone, and language mechanics. The state provides specific descriptors and benchmark pieces of student work by which to determine how often (extensively, frequently, sometimes, rarely) an author succeeds in each of these dimensions. Indeed, these categories form the staple of traditional analysis. Because I already had a sense of where each of my students was operating in each category, I thought that it would be easy to transfer what I knew onto the code sheets. Complications, however, rendered the collection and assessment incredibly cumbersome.

Vermont Portfolio Requirements

At the eighth grade level, the State Department of Education requires several writing samples from English, a letter explaining the writing process behind a "best piece," as well as three prose pieces from subject areas other than language arts. My students are normally required to write weekly for their personal writing folders so that by February they have built a file from which to choose pieces to bring to the critique sessions. At the beginning of this past year, I had also asked students to save their essays from other subjects in anticipation of the portfolios. From time to time I reminded them, but for the most part students did not take heed. Therefore, come February, when they were to select papers from their writing folders to place in the state portfolio, many students had a paucity of prose pieces from other subject areas.

The class discussion that emerged was enlightening for me. Even though many students had written some thought-provoking and insightful academic essays, they did not care enough to save them as they had saved their creative writing. "Why didn't you make us keep them?" or, "We don't care about that," they complained. As a result, some students grabbed "any old piece" that they could find simply to fulfill the requirement. One student commented, "In the beginning everything about the portfolio was distant and eventually forgotten. I knew the requirements, but the whole business seemed unimportant ..."

In stark contrast to the number of prose pieces from other subject areas, almost all students had large files of creative writing to choose from. The state-required letters about process that accompanied their self-designated "best pieces" were replete with specific detail, a sense of pride and ownership:

Dear Reader,

I suppose one could say that the inspiration to write this story came out of nowhere. I began typing and the words which ran onto the page seemed to fit. My thoughts seemed to spew forth and it was difficult for my hands to type at the same speed that my mind was going ... I knew that I wanted my writing to be controlled and not free and flaky. I limited my amount of description and countless adverbs ...

My reason for not including too much detailed description about each of the characters was to make the story seem like a sudden flash of a different life, as seen through the eyes of a stranger. I feel that I succeeded in this aspect of my writing style. I feel that writing this way also leads the reader to make decisions for him or herself. I left much of the different characters' history up to the reader's imagination. I not only left the history to the reader to determine, but also left out specifics that might have been extremely necessary if this had been a novel or another style of writing. ...

Overall I feel very proud of my story. I feel that I have discovered something new about my potential to try new techniques and styles. I hope that my story comes across as something of interest and something to ponder for the reader.

Sincerely,

Moriah Karlan

Dear Reader,

I selected this piece of poetry because it meant the most to me. One reason I wrote this piece was because it is a way to let my anger and hate out. Another reason is because I like writing about gloomy things that might happen to another person. If it does happen to others that might read it the people will probably want to express their feelings in the same way. I hope you like this piece as much as I do.

Sincerely,

Craig Lincoln

Dear Reader,

This story was a dramatic change from the other stories I have written in the past three years. It could be described as the product of breaking out of a common mold.

... Description can sometimes be the main asset to the story. It has many ways of appearing. Description can subtly give a word or phrase more appeal or can stand basically on its own. These two are pretty well covered in my story. 'In this dream she walked down a path of wilted brush and debris where she saw a single black rose encased in fire.' This sentence is full of description, yet it isn't drowned out by it. In another sentence, 'She picked up the emerald stem with admiration,' the description is very subtle.

Any way you look at the story, the one thing that is obvious, is the fable-like appearance. In a way, fantasy is like fact. Even though unreal things are happening, real things about the writer, the reader, or the present day world are surfaced ...

What it boils down to is that this story is a milestone in my writing.

> *Sincerely,*
>
> *Anna Dumonde*

Not all of the student responses to the portfolio came directly from class assignments or personal writing. For some the act of formalizing their collection of work for the state prompted them to complete creative pieces that would never have been finished otherwise. "I knew how to assess writing before this work, but I lacked the motivation to do it on the large scale used for an entire portfolio. The most important thing I've learned is that I can complete stories if I take the time." This particular student substantially redrafted her best piece eight times before including it in the portfolio.

Even though a lengthy process preceded the completion of almost all of the writing pieces, little material evidence remained. I was curious as to why. My students, because they were writing on computers, found it hard to save every draft, and, according to them, successive savings of files on the computer makes keeping things less important. Composing at the computer allows for instant rewrite; printing hard copies of each step is wasteful and time-consuming. They also reminded me that reflecting on each step of their writing was my concern, not theirs.

Questions after the First Year

Going through the first year of a state-wide portfolio assessment, I have come to see the benefits of formal collection for me and for my students. The state requirement has set an official tone to which students respond seriously. It is now for us (teachers and students) to figure out why students hold their personal writing more dearly than they do their academic essay assignments. Is this due to the nature of content writing or to the types of questions being posed? In addition, I need to rethink the need for computer-generated drafts, and outside examiners need to check their assumption that if drafts aren't present the students have not gone through a process.

I would like to see the state of Vermont continue its portfolio initiative. Many of the difficulties of assessing and recording that my class and I encountered this year will be smoothed out. But it is my belief that we would accumulate a more genuine portfolio if student scores were not aggregated and reported publicly. Public report of portfolio assessment scores changes the basic nature of the portfolio record-keeping and puts my classroom goals of open discussion and experimentation at cross-purposes with the state goal of accountability. There is a shift from examining student process to measuring teacher performance that occurs with ranking. Despite state disclaimers and an "official" acknowledgement that teachers at grades four and eight are only partially responsible for the development of student writing, intense pressure is placed on teachers at these grade levels to have stellar portfolios. This is implied pressure, motivated by the public report, and manifests itself in high anxiety among many teachers who spend countless hours in the preparation and scoring of the portfolios.

Furthermore, this implied judgment of teachers makes it less likely that students will be allowed a completely free choice about which pieces to select for the portfolio. I found myself steering three students away from selections that they would have made in favor of pieces that I knew would receive higher scores. In addition, I asked students to continue redrafting academic writing assignments that had already been submitted and graded by me or other teachers. I saw a similar pattern in some of the portfolios I read at a regional conference. Most teachers will not publicly admit that they do this, but it is inherent when teacher evaluation gets mixed with student assessment. The question then becomes "Whose work is it?"

The Writing Prompt

I think that an alternative for accountability might lie in the writing prompt. In addition to the portfolios, Vermont requires that all students in grades four and eight complete a ninety-minute writing session about a topic which is determined by a state committee of teachers. Students and classroom teachers do not know the topic in advance. When they write, students are allowed to use resource materials, but they may not confer with teachers or peers. As I watched my class take the writing prompt, I was impressed by how engrossed they became in their work. Students wrote and revised for the full ninety minutes on a topic that I thought would not engage them: "As children we all had toys and playthings. Some of these were expensive items and some were not, like an old beat-up pan with a wooden spoon. Think about the toy or plaything that was a particular favorite and write about it. Show how and why it was such a favorite." After a reminder that they could be as creative as they liked and that the story they wrote did not have to be true, the students relaxed and had fun with the topic. Only three out of twenty-five students reported that they hated the writing task. Another ten remained neutral. Despite these objections or non-reactions, the writing that grew from this assignment was fresh and alive with both description and personal voice. I was pleased to read the essays and recognize that these prompts fairly represented the writing abilities of my students.

The drawbacks of using the prompt as an assessment tool are that it depends on having a valid topic and it prohibits conferencing, a mainstay of mine and many teachers' writing programs. Despite this, I think that the state of Vermont should use the prompt for its accountability needs and allow teachers to use portfolios to track student progress in an honest, unsanitized manner. Assessment loses its authenticity when it turns its face and becomes public accountability.

An English Department Portfolio Project

Jan Bergamini

This portfolio project, led by a California teacher, grew to include grades nine through twelve over a four-year period. During that time, portfolios became the vehicle that took teachers on a journey in which they looked at the content and purposes of writing and teaching for students and themselves.

Beginning in the fall of 1988, English teachers at Mt. Diablo High School in Concord, California, began working with student writing portfolios. This experience changed the way we see our students as writers and as people. Because of our work with portfolios, we have altered the way we teach writing as well as the ways in which we talk to each other as members of an English department.

Mt. Diablo is the oldest high school in Contra Costa County, dating back to the early part of this century. Today, the 1,200 students reflect California's rich multi-ethnic population: 28% Hispanic, 12% African-American, 10% Asian, and 48% Caucasian. We have the largest English as a Second Language program in our school district and we offer sheltered classes in the four major content areas.

Each year of this four-year portfolio project looked like this. Sometime early in October, after the insanity of the opening of school had subsided, we met for half a day to decide what the purposes and contents of this portfolio project would be. In February we met again for half a day to read "live" student papers from the categories or types we had selected to go into the portfolios. We read for what was good and strong in these papers, and began to develop the criteria we would use in assessing our students' writing. In May we met for two days, off campus, to read, assess, and respond to our students' portfolios.

When I think back to that first October in 1988, our first year of the portfolio project, a picture is framed in my mind: Ten earnest men and women are trying to articulate not only what we teach when it comes to writing, but why we teach it the way we teach it. Because we, like most other teachers, rarely have time to discuss questions like these, it is a painful but gradually liberating process. There are long silences. People tentatively express a point of view, immediately followed by the pro forma apology, "Well, I don't mean that quite as I described it." We are struggling with the most important question we will have to answer in the four years of our project. That answer, once arrived at, will serve as our guidepost in creating this Mt. Diablo portfolio project: What are our purposes for having students create writing portfolios as part of our English curriculum?

When we finally begin to open up to one another, twenty-seven purposes tumble out, filling the chalkboard, ranging from students feeling a pride in their writing to having the portfolios serve as a way to "place" students in their next year's English class. We have student purposes and teacher purposes — too many purposes.

After much discussion and examination of our approaches to teaching writing, we decide on these three purposes for using portfolios: to empower students and to motivate all students as writers; to design a coherent four-year writing program; and to serve as an end-of-course culminating activity.

The second purpose didn't last into November, since department members were justifiably suspicious of a statement so rigid and prison-like, implying certain types or modes of writing must be taught at certain grade levels. We talked; we argued; we agreed on a revised second purpose: to assess our teaching of writing.

Decisions about the contents of that first year's portfolio were arrived at rather quickly. We asked the ninth grade teachers to share writing assignments, and we listed them on the board. There were so many possibilities and they were of such variety that we ran out of room. We agreed that probably five papers would be a manageable number and, by a process of elimination, decided on a daily writing, a memory piece, a descriptive writing, a position or opinion paper, a wild card (a paper of any kind that the student chooses to submit), and a letter of introduction to the portfolio.

That first year we made some other basic decisions. We would not have every student in the school keep portfolios—that seemed an overwhelming task. We would, however, follow one group of students, the graduating class of 1992, from freshman to senior year. Would they improve or would they, as some of us secretly feared, show their best writing as ninth graders and go downhill from that point on? We also wanted to test the feasibility of four-year portfolios in a school with a tremendous turnover of students, a continuously revolving door of admissions and transfers.

The most important decision we made that first year came sometime in March. Unlike in previous years, our department meetings now included time to discuss writing and how we taught it. At this meeting my colleague, Maxine Emerson, looked up from a paper she was reading and said, "You know, if our first and most important purpose is to empower and motivate our students as writers, then we are going to have to respond to them. We're going to have to write them a letter or something. We can't just give them a grade." After the shouts of, "Are you crazy? We'd never have time!" quieted, we agreed she was absolutely right. We would have to write to our students in their portfolios.

Here are excerpts from some of our early responses to the writers:

Your papers read as if they were written by a real person.

I like your sense of outrage at the terrible things in life and how they should be changed by 'someone.' How about you?

> *Yes, you are something of a guinea pig and am I glad we found you. You are planning to be a writer, aren't you?*

As this first year ended we were filled with a sense of what we had begun — an ongoing conversation with our students about their writing.

Because of what we had learned from the previous year, at our second October meeting in 1989 we changed the contents of the portfolio. Both freshman teachers and students had felt constrained by the writing types, because it took several of each kind in order to be able to make selections. So, instead of writing types, we broadened the portfolio's contents to writing strategies. The contents for that second year would be responding to literature, comparing and contrasting, reflecting, stating and supporting an opinion, a wild card, and an introductory letter.

We kept our initial purposes but added to them. We wanted our students to see growth from their freshman year to the sophomore year, and the portfolio would be the perfect way to do that. We learned from that first reading that our students were primarily first draft writers and were not revising. We agreed to encourage and consciously emphasize revision in our teaching.

In their sophomore year, as students continued to write and select pieces for their portfolios, they had many chances to reflect on their changes and growth as writers, many "baby freshman" or "stupid sophomore" papers to wonder at.

When my three classes of sophomores were given their freshman portfolios for the first time, I asked them to respond to two questions. First, how did they feel after looking at their freshman writings? And second, what could they say about any changes they saw in themselves as writers?

Here are some of the sophomore "light bulbs" that went off:

> Monica: *When I looked at last year's writings and when I looked at this year's writings I could see how many more drafts I have. I developed my writings a lot further this year. I also noticed that in both years it seems like my descriptive essays are the best.*

Ron: *Was that really me who wrote those papers?! I can't believe it! My writing style has changed so much within the last year or so. Back then I was so descriptive, with a little humor added to my work to liven things up! But now, I think I'm more serious about what I write and to read it is like a rainy, Sunday morning with no electricity at all while your friends are out. In other words, it's BORING.*

Amber: *I express myself more clearly now and get straight to the point in my writing. I write more of what I want to say, not what I think the reader would like to hear.*

Cheryl: *Reading over last year's portfolio was kinda strange. I read things that I had totally forgotten about. Some, I couldn't believe I wrote! I feel, though, my writing is some-what better this year and I hope to improve it more. You can't do well if you can't write and express your self well. I even bought a thesaurus with over 1300 words in it!*

Darron: *As I compared this year's writings to last year's writings, I found out that I have grown as a writer. My papers make more sense now, they express more thought and feelings, and they also make their point in a much more clear and concise manner.*

As we moved into the third year of the project, we asked the entire junior class to write their English teachers letters telling us how they felt about portfolios and what they would like to see included. We received over 250 letters, and did they tell us!

We learned that categories, types, genres, and labels often stultify students' efforts. They said, "Some of my best writings don't fit into your categories." They said, "Maybe it's just me, but I wasn't happy with the guidelines." They said, "I just can't force my best writing (poetry) into a comparison/contrast category." They said, "Please have fewer literature responses because students often have no response to literature at all."

We listened to our students, as we were learning to do, and once again changed the contents but not the purposes. As we had done previously, we broadened the contents and decided on these: my personal best, my most imaginative, a paper from another discipline, a paper that shows process and revision, a piece that shows potential for further work, a paper that states and supports an opinion, and a reflective letter that focuses on the self as writer.

The portfolio would have five pieces. One must show process and revision and one must be an opinion.

When we met in May, 1991 to read these junior portfolios, we agreed to look for general writing abilities such as development of ideas, personal voice, use of language, organization appropriate to the writing, and ability to revise. During this reading we also took the opportunity to read at random some three-year portfolios and write a description of what we found in terms of growth, student reflection, and student attitudes towards using portfolios. In addition, we asked teachers from other disciplines to read with us. We called it the "English Invitational" and, with our principal's support, substitutes were provided so that teachers from science, ESL, and social studies could read with us. Already reading with us were our learning opportunity program coordinator, our Chapter I coordinator, and a variety of district office people, including the assistant superintendent of secondary education, the assistant superintendent of curriculum, and our language arts consultant.

The fourth year again began with our seniors writing letters to their English teachers telling what they wanted their senior portfolio to be. As we met for our last October meeting, the senior opinion was clear: let us have full freedom to select what we want. They were adamant about it:

> Grace: *I really wish that this year's portfolio would be filled with writings of intense feeling.*

> Caroline: *I want this year's contents to be freely up to me. I wish I could have the College Boards read some of this*

writing because I truly believe it reflects the true me, from my morals to my sense of humor.

Tom: *I recommend we are allowed to put our own writings, not assigned by you, but writings that we do on our own at home where our true feelings come out onto the paper.*

Diana: *Perhaps we could make our own categories.*

Jennifer: *I would like to include a reflective work based on our past portfolios. The broadness of the topics is very helpful.*

Pete: *Let us choose our best papers — no labels or categories.*

We took Pete's advice, and here are the instructions we gave to these veteran portfolio writers for their last, senior portfolio:

INSTRUCTIONS FOR WHAT TO INCLUDE:
1. Introductory Letter.
2. As you look at your portfolio, how does it mirror you as an individual, showing your growth and change as a person and as a writer?
3. Explain how the six pieces you have selected this year show your range as a writer.
4. Write about your experience with this portfolio project.
5. Table of Contents.
6. An explanation of each piece of writing in the portfolio (assignment, focus of writing).
7. Six pieces that show your range as a writer.

As we met to read portfolios for the last time in May, 1992, there was a certain nostalgia, for something good was coming to an end.

Well, not really to an end, for we had decided earlier in the year that we would continue to use portfolios, perhaps somewhat differently, but continue nonetheless, and they would be the focus of our English department.

Looking ahead to the fifth year, knowing there are student portfolios waiting for me, I have done some thinking about how I will use them in my classroom.

In the first weeks I plan to get students into their portfolios, have them reflect on the writing represented there, and ask them to set one or two goals they want to work on in their writing. Students new to the school or those without portfolios can do a writing during this time and begin a portfolio.

I plan to use the portfolio early on to help create criteria for good writing. Perhaps students can select a piece from the portfolio to share in a writing group, asking readers to look for what is good in the writing and then come up with a list to share with the rest of the class. I will post a representative list of criteria of good writing for the class to refer to during the quarter, with emphasis on showing, concrete writing with a strong voice. Depending on the grade level, style, tone, and other more sophisticated elements of writing will be incorporated. In this way, early in the year and in a natural manner, students will develop a beginning vocabulary to talk about their writing.

I will use the portfolio as a basis for teaching revision. I will have students select one piece with which they aren't quite satisfied and have them revise it in terms of content, ideas, examples, grammar, and mechanics. Here is a checklist I have used for the last three years to help my students in their revision:

CHECKLIST

As you revise your papers use this simple checklist to help you.

1. _____ read this piece, and we talked about it.

2. I revised this piece of writing as follows:
   - Length: I expanded my ideas; I wrote more.
   - Content: I provided more support through examples.
   - Editing: I removed repetition, made sentences more concise, tightened paragraphs.
   - Mechanics: I corrected for spelling, grammar. and punctuation.

3. The writing goals I worked on in this revised piece are:

I will have students in and out of their portfolios throughout the year, making initial selections of best pieces, reflecting on these as the year progresses, adding pieces, replacing some previous selections with pieces the writer considers better, thus continuing to develop a rationale and criteria for best pieces. Each quarter students will submit a working portfolio containing a limited number of pieces with an introductory letter. Each piece will probably have brainstorming, idea-generating scribbles, rough drafts, and final draft. Included will be reflections the students have written during and after the writing is completed. For example,"What are you having difficulty with in this piece?" or "What is especially strong in this piece that you want me to look for?"

There will be response from other readers. Before I read the portfolios, writing groups will have read and responded to the portfolio in a letter to the writer. I will also respond, probably in a brief letter that will be tied to the writer's introductory letter. I may, because I teach five classes of approximately 30-33 students each, combine my personal remarks with some sort of a checklist to make this task more manageable. I did this with my two senior classes as part of their first semester final as well as with their final senior portfolio. It worked quite well, but a checklist and grade is not enough. The personal response of the letter is absolutely essential. I will definitely make this working portfolio a significant part of the quarter grade.

I will also use some of the materials I developed over the past four years and I will keep a copy of the checklist I used with my senior portfolios.

Often, as part of our four-year experiment in portfolio assessment, we asked our students to write back to the teacher who had read and responded to their portfolios. These student letters taught us a great deal about the art of writing responses to students.

• Responding to the student writer is a difficult art, and I will refer often to what I have learned from students.

> Gary: *Finally I feel I have found someone that understands the important parts of my writings. In my descriptive writing of the little girl you understand the feeling I was trying to get across to the reader. It's exciting to know that I could do this and inspires me to put even more effort into my writing.*

> Jennifer: *Thank you for your kind and helpful comments. You took the writings the way I intended. These papers all have a great deal of feeling in them. This makes them special to me.*

> Jason: *You grabbed a hold of my good writings and commented on them. I appreciate that you helped me realize conclusions can make or break a story.*

> Monica: *You were very specific which helped me because I could look back and understand your criticisms and suggestions for improvement. I like to hear and get opinions on what is weak in my writings.*

> Jody: *The problem with your response to my portfolio was there was almost absolutely nothing positive written. I*

walked away feeling like I was a horrible writer and had a long way to go before I would be considered 'good.' The helpful hints are great but I also need some assurance to know that I am on the right track.

Susan: *I was glad you understood what I was trying to say. I'm not good at putting my feelings down. You're right. I do leave out a lot of information which is what my problem is. Now I know what to work on for next year.*

• Students need to have a choice in what they write.

Kathy: *I think teachers should instruct their students to write more and on many different topics and periodically have them revise certain papers. That way they won't have to scramble as much when choosing papers, and they will have a wide variety to choose from.*

Monica: *If I had to change anything with this portfolio project it would be the categorizing of our pieces. This limited us too much, but I can see how freshmen might need some guiding to show their range, unlike us fully matured seniors, of course. Ha, Ha!*

Scott: *During my junior year I learned structure but the price paid must have been the fun that the two previous years were. My writing felt squeezed within the limits and while it is a good thing that I learned some form and structure that year, I found it difficult to express myself.*

John: *I am amazed at myself. I have a lot of writings to submit. Kina strains the brain, don't it?*

• The classroom environment needs to encourage risk-taking.

Monica: *The most important thing I have learned which I am sure was not one of the main intentions of the project was that for me to write my best I must relax and take a chance. This part of me was stifled in one of my years and reflected severely in my works.*

• A grade or a "score" alone does not encourage a student writer.

Jennifer: *Having someone respond to my writings every year has given me the opportunity to see what types of writings I do that people like. I also get the strong constructive criticism that helps me to develop as a writer. The personal comments on my writings give me advice and support. For me the personal connection that occurs between the reader and my writings is what I valued most.*

• To be most effective portfolios must be integrated into the writing instruction throughout the year.

Diana: *Some teachers need to get more involved and spend more time to get a variety of writings for the students, Also, writing in a rush never turns out great writing.*

• Students can and need to reflect to recognize growth in their writing.

Rio: *Part, (I think a big part) of high school is growing. Not just growing, maturing. It is a treasure to have physical evidence of that growth. What the project gave us is the beginning step of our creative self, as well as an on going record of the maturation of what we created.*

Ron: *Back when I was an 'eeney weenie' kid (about the sixth grade), my knack for writing finally paid off as a short story*

I wrote for English class got school recognition. I never really thought I was that good. I couldn't see myself as a writer back then. I couldn't see my progress as a writer, either. This was because my teacher kept my best stories and the other stuff I never thought about saving. Years passed by, my stories were graded and ended up as charcoal lighter or 'three point' attempts into the waste basket. But things changed for the better when I enrolled into high school and this portfolio project began. I could see my style of writing over the years. I could see what areas of writing I've improved in and what needs working on. When I looked into the mirror, alas, there stood staring back at me, a writer.

Diana: *Until I started this portfolio project I never even looked at my writing after it was graded. That didn't help me to see what I was doing wrong. Reading papers after a while had passed I could easily spot things that I never noticed before.*

Hali: *The whole idea of your writings from high school as a kind of scrapbook is an incredible way for kids to actually see how they and their writing have matured. I myself am able to read what I wrote my freshman year, and remember how I felt, what I was thinking when I wrote it, who my friends were, and who the crush of the month was.*

Kathy: *Just being able to see how my mind has wandered and developed over a four year period makes the project worthwhile.*

• Portfolios can and do work with all kinds of students.

Carlos: *This is my second year in Mt. Diablo and in the U.S. Too bad that I didn't start here as a freshman, because I could have seen how far I've gotten in four years. But I guess two years could prove a little something about my writing.*

157

Delfino: *I opened my portfolio and looked through all my sophomore writings. I could still feel the strong feeling of missing my homeland, friends, and the feeling of loneliness. At that time, I was a newcomer in the US. When I first went to school here I could not even write essays in English well ... Now I can see myself as a mature, skillful writer.*

• For good writing and portfolios to flourish, the classroom environment must be an interactive and supportive one.

Grace: *I remember the first time I stepped into an English classroom here in America. It wasn't like the ones I had back in my homeland. There was talking. And talking ... and talking.. an interaction going on between teacher and students. It was a bond that seemed so natural to them that it made me feel uneasy, for I never knew such bonding.*

As a result of this portfolio project we came to know this class of students more than most. We learned to value their opinions and insights about writing, how they felt about it, where they liked to write, what kinds of writing they preferred, the kind of classroom environment they appreciated when it came to writing, and what they needed from us as teachers of writing. This information was gathered as we worked with portfolios in our individual classrooms, as the students reflected on that process over the four years, and from the letters they wrote introducing their portfolios for us to read each May.

I know that my teaching and my perspective on the students I teach will never be the same again. They have taught me so much, and the forum for that knowledge was the portfolio project we began four years ago.

Dear Reader,

I would like to put a special thanks in here to the teachers who have helped me out when I needed it. Even if it was in the smallest way, it helped. You know who you are.

Dear Reader,

To all the English teachers in general I want you to realize that even though we groan when we have to do an assignment, usually when we are done we have something to be proud of and part of it came from your hard work and concerns. Being a teacher is a hard thing, especially at this school but don't let down. You are all doing a great job.

Contributors

Jan Bergamini, a twenty-five year veteran in the classroom, teaches English at Mt. Diablo High School in Concord, California. As English department chairperson, she led her colleagues through a four-year writing portfolio project. During the project, her sophomore class appeared on a CBS special education program. She was county Teacher of the Year in 1991. A Bay Area Writing Project teacher consultant, she has given workshops on portfolios throughout the state and in several other Western states. She has also been a singer for forty years, beginning in junior high school. Presently she sings, along with fourteen others, in a Bay Area chamber chorus called "Encore."

Lois Brandts has been an elementary teacher for over twenty years. Currently, she teaches first grade at Hollister Elementary in Goleta, California. She has served in various roles with the South Coast Writing Project at the University of California in Santa Barbara: teacher consultant, teacher researcher, associate director and co-director. A presenter at county, state, and national conferences, she works with colleagues on strategies for teaching language minority students. Among the professional organizations to which she belongs is the National Association for the Perpetuation and Preservation of Storytelling.

Joni Chancer teaches fourth and fifth grade at Oak Hills Elementary in Agoura, California. Now in her twentieth year of teaching, she began her career in Melbourne, Australia, where she and her ESL students participated together in the pioneering days of whole language movement. Among her published articles is a fiction piece taken from her life in Australia. A co-director of the South Coast Writing Project, she has appeared on an Educational Television Network program on portfolios. She is also the recipient of stacks of letters from former students who tell her they are still writing and are especially fond of the stories they wrote in the fourth grade.

Mary Kay Deen has spent most of her twenty-eight years of teaching working with first graders. She teaches at North Bay Elementary School in Bay St. Louis, Mississippi, and is a teacher consultant with the South Mississippi Writing Project in Hattisburg. She belongs to ten professional organizations, including the National Council of Teachers of English, the International Readings Association, and the Mississippi Geographic Alliance. A charter member of the statewide Writing Project Portfolio Task Force, she has published articles for her teaching colleagues in Mississippi. She receives, she says, visits every night from Oneofa, a maskless raccoon who lives under her house and inspires her also to be one of a kind.

Dixie G. Dellinger teaches English at Burns High School in Lawndale, North Carolina. A twenty-eight year veteran in the classroom, she has also served as subject area coordinator for English and social studies. She has published over fifteen articles on the teaching of writing, along with her book *Out of the Heart: How to Design Writing Assignments for High School Courses*. A teacher consultant with the UNC Charlotte Writing Project, she has conducted workshops in eight states. She is a member of the National Writing Project National Board of Advisors and second vice president of the North Carolina English Teachers Association. She keeps her childhood home at Flat Rock, NC, where she goes with her husband to relax and watch the mountains wear down.

John Dorroh, a science teacher at West Point High School in West Point, Mississippi, has taught for seventeen years and during that time received three different "Teacher of the Year" awards. He is a teacher consultant with the Mississippi Writing/Thinking Institute at Mississippi State University and a member of the statewide Writing Project Portfolio Task Force. He has directed school plays, coached tennis, and coordinated district science fairs. He is the author of several articles and grant proposals, and he is also an avid letter writer, exchanging letters with over one hundred correspondents in twenty countries. He is a published poet.

Nancy Green has been teaching for twenty-three years. She is currently a fifth grade teacher at Parkway Elementary in St. Joseph, Missouri, and an active teacher consultant with the Writing Project at St. Joseph. She has published several articles, including "A Quilt for a Grandchild" in *Quilting International*. A first-time grandmother, she and her husband are celebrating their thirty-third wedding anniversary this year. Both of her children are also teachers.

Bob Ingalls teaches English and speech at Mt. Vernon High School in Alexandria, Virginia, and is co-director of the Northern Virginia Writing Project at George Mason University. He has written several articles for his colleagues, including "Flag Me Down and Tell Me Where You Want to Go: Hackin' with Atwell," a piece about cab driving and teaching. His teaching philosophy is to listen to the passengers, take them where they want to go, and always use cab driving language. His portfolio philosophy is to concentrate on the issues and conditions that allow students to make the folder more than just a folder.

Joyce Jones, an English teacher for twenty-four years, is currently a member of the Mt. Vernon High School faculty in Alexandria, Virginia. She belongs to eight professional organizations, one of which is the Northern Virginia Writing Project. As a teacher consultant, she has taught inservice classes at George Mason University, served on the Summer Institute staff, and assumed the lifelong position of co-chair of the local Language and Literacy Conference. She keeps in contact with a great many former students who send her wedding and baby announcements with the expectation that she will respond with the appropriate gift — a book.

Jane Juska has been a high school English teacher for thirty-two years, the last twenty-three years of which she has been teaching at Ygnacio Valley High School in Concord, California. As a teacher consultant with the Bay Area Writing Project at the University of California, Berkeley, she has conducted workshops in eight states as well as in Japan and Okinawa. She is a member of the National Writing Project National Board of Advisors. Author of more than a dozen articles, she won first prize from Education Writers of America for the best article published in special interest/trade publications. This article, "The Unteachables," first appeared in the *NWP/CSW Quarterly*. She also won the best field trips award, presented by the 1990 senior class at Ygnacio Valley.

Susan Reed has seventeen years of classroom experience. She teaches at El Cerrito High School in El Cerrito, California, and is a teacher consultant with the Bay Area Writing Project, University of California, Berkeley. She is also a coordinator for the National Writing Project Urban Sites Writing Network. Author of several articles on the teaching of writing, she received the 1988 *English Journal* Best Writing Award for her article, "Logs: Keeping an Open Mind," in the February 88 *EJ*. She says that, through writing along with her students, she is only now "beginning to figure out what I'm doing."

Mary Ann Smith is executive director of the California Writing Project and co-director of the National Writing Project. A former director of the Bay Area Writing Project, she began her association with the Project at UC Berkeley in 1974 as a junior high school English teacher. She has also taught high school English. Author of several articles on the teaching and assessment of writing and on the contributions of National Writing Project teachers, she is co-author, with Sandra Murphy, of *Writing Portfolios: A Bridge* *from Teaching to Assessment* (Pippin, 1991). She always follows the advice of her writing group.

Fern Tavalin has been a classroom teacher for eight years, most recently at the middle school level. A former elementary teacher at Putney Central in Putney, Vermont, she is now a doctoral candidate at the University of Massachusetts Elementary Teacher Education Program. Her dissertation focuses on voice and writing through the telling of personal stories. As a teacher scholar interested in the effects of collaboration and group discussion on reading, writing, and thinking, she also works with a group of fifth and sixth graders on writing radio plays.

Tamsie West, a fifteen-year English teacher, presently teaches at Magee High School in Magee, Mississippi, in the south central part of the state. She is a teacher consultant with the Mississippi Writing/Thinking Institute at Mississippi State University and a member of the statewide Portfolio Task Force. In 1991, she was district Teacher of the Year. She is a founder of the Black Rose Theatre Company and she directs one play a year. Her current production is *Grease*.

Miriam Ylvisaker is the editor of *The NWP/CSW Quarterly*. She formerly taught high school English in the Oakland Public Schools, and her articles and stories have appeared in *California English, English Journal, Phi Delta Kappan, Descant, Kansas Quarterly,* and *The Progressive*. She was in the first Bay Area (later to become National) Writing Project Summer Institute in 1974.

Selected Bibliography

Books and Monographs

Belanoff, P., & Dickson, M. (Eds.). (1991). *Portfolios: Process and product*. Portsmouth, NH: Heinemann, Boynton/Cook.

Berlak, H., Newmann, F. M., Adams, E., Archbald, D. A., Burgess, T., Raven, J., & Romberg, T. A. (1992). *Toward a new science of educational testing and assessment*. Albany, NY: State University of New York Press.

Gill, K. (Ed.). (1993). *Process and portfolios in writing instruction*. Urbana, IL: National Council of Teachers of English.

Graves, D., & Sunstein, B. S. (Eds.). (1992). *Portfolio portraits*. Portsmouth, NH: Heinemann, Boynton/Cook.

Hewitt, G. (1989). *Vermont portfolio assessment project*. Montpelier, VT: Vermont State Department of Education.

Mitchell, R. (1992). *Testing for learning*. New York: Macmillan Free Press.

Mumme, J. (1990). *Portfolio assessment in mathematics*. Santa Barbara: University of California, California Mathematics Project.

Murphy, S., & Smith, M. A. (1991). *Writing portfolios: A bridge from teaching to assessment*. Markham, Ontario: Pippin Press Limited.

Stenmark, J. K. (1989). *Assessment alternatives in mathematics*. Berkeley: University of California, EQUALS and California Mathematics Council.

Tierney, R. J., Carter, M. A., & Desai, L. E. (1991). *Portfolio assessment in the reading-writing classroom.* Norwood, MA: Christopher-Gordon.

Yancey, K. B. (Ed.). (1992). *Portfolios in the writing classroom.* Urbana, IL: National Council of Teachers of English.

Articles

Adams, D. M., & Hamm, M. E. (1992). Portfolio assessment and social studies. *Social Education, 56* (2), 103-105.

Arter, J. A., & Spandel, V. (1992). NCME instructional module: Using portfolios of student work in instruction and assessment. *Educational Measurement: Issues and Practice, 11* (1), 36-44.

Bingham, A. (1988). Using writing folders to document student progress. In T. Newkirk & N. Atwell (Eds.), *Understanding writing: Ways of observing, learning and teaching* (2nd ed.) (pp. 216-225). Portsmouth, NH: Heinemann, Boynton/Cook.

Camp, R. (in press). Assessment in the context of schools and school change. In H. Marshall (Ed.), *Supporting student learning: Roots of educational change.* Norwood, NJ: Ablex.

Camp, R. (1993). The place of portfolios in our changing views of writing assessment. In R. Bennett & W. Ward (Eds.), *Construction versus choice in cognitive measurement* (pp. 183-212). Hillsdale, NJ: Lawrence Erlbaum Associates.

Camp, R. (1990). Thinking together about portfolios. *The NWP/CSW Quarterly, 12* (2), 8-14, 27.

Collins, A. (1990). Portfolios for assessing student learning in science: A new name for a familiar idea? In A. B. Champagne, B. E. Lovitts, & B. E. Callinger (Eds.), *Assessment in the service of instruction.* Washington, DC: American Association for the Advancement of Science.

Cooper, W., & Brown, B. J. (1992). Using portfolios to empower student writers. *English Journal, 81* (2), 40-5.

Educational Testing Service. (1989). *The student writer: An endangered species?* Focus 23. Princeton, NJ: Educational Testing Service.

Erickson, M. (1992). Developing student confidence to evaluate writing. *The NWP/CSW Quarterly, 14,* 7-9.

Ferguson, S. (1992). Zeroing in on math abilities. *Learning, 21 (3),* 38-41.

Galleher, D. (1987). Assessment in context: Toward a national writing project model. *The NWP/CSW Quarterly, 9* (3), 5-7.

Gearhart, M., Herman, J. L., Baker, E. L., & Whittaker, A. K. (1992). *Writing portfolios at the elementary level: A study of methods for writing assessment.* Technical Report No. 337. Los Angeles: University of California, Center for the Study of Evaluation.

Gelfer, J. I., & Perkins, P. G. (1992). Constructing student portfolios: A process and product that fosters communication with families. *Day Care Early Education,* 20 (2), 9-13.

Gitomer, D. H., Grosh, S., & Price, K. (1992). Portfolio culture in arts education. *Art Education, 45* (1), 7-15.

Hamm, M., & Adams, D. M. (1991). Portfolio: It's not just for artists anymore. *The Science Teacher 58,* 18-21.

Hansen, J. (1992). Evaluation: "My portfolio shows who I am." *The NWP/CSW Quarterly, 14* (1), 5-6, 9.

Hansen, J. (1992). Literacy portfolios emerge. *Reading Teacher, 45* (4), 604-607.

Harp, B. (in press). Classroom assessment. In Purves, A. (Ed.) *Encyclopedia of English studies and language arts.* Urbana, IL: National Council of Teachers of English.

Hebert, E. A. (1992). Portfolios invite reflection—from students *and* staff. *Educational Leadership, 49* (8), 58-61.

Howard, K. (1990). Making the writing portfolio real. *The NWP/ CSW Quarterly, 12* (2), 4-7, 27.

Jordan, S. (in press). Portfolio assessment. In Purves, A. (Ed.) *Encyclopedia of English studies and language arts.* Urbana, IL: National Council of Teachers of English.

Kirby, D., & Kuykendall, C. (1991). Growing thinkers. *Mind matters: Teaching for thinking.* Portsmouth, NH: Boynton/Cook, Heinemann.

Lucas, C. K. (1988). Toward ecological evaluation, Part 1. *The NWP/CSW Quarterly, 10* (1), 1-2, 12-17.

Lucas, C. K. (1988). Toward ecological evaluation. Part 2. *The NWP/CSW Quarterly, 10* (2), 4-10.

Moss, P. A., Beck, J. S., Ebbs, C., Matson, B., Muchmore, J., Steele, D., Taylor, C., & Herter, R. (1992). Portfolios, accountability, and an interpretative approach to validity. *Educational Measurement: Issues and Practice, 11* (3), 12-21.

Murphy, S., & Smith, M. A. (1990). Talking about portfolios. *The NWP/CSW Quarterly, 12* (2).

Paulson, F. L., Paulson, P. R., & Meyer, C. A. (1991). What makes a portfolio a portfolio? *Educational Leadership, 48* (5), 60-63.

Purves, A. (in press). Achievement testing and literature. In Purves, A. (Ed.) *Encyclopedia of English studies and language arts.* Urbana, IL: National Council of Teachers of English.

Rief, L. (1992). Finding the value in evaluation: Portfolios. *Seeking diversity: Language arts with adolescents.* Portsmouth, NH: Heinemann, Boynton/Cook.

Rief, L. (1990). Finding the value in evaluation: Self-assessment in a middle school classroom. *Educational Leadership, 47* (6), 24-29.

Roemer, M., Schultz, L. M., & Durst, R. K. (1991, December). Portfolios and the process of change. *College Composition and Communication, 42* (4), 455-469.

Simmons, J. (1990). Portfolios as large-scale assessment. *Language Arts, 67* (3), 262-267.

Smith, M.A. (in press). Assessment and staff development. In Purves, A. (Ed.) *Encyclopedia of English studies and language arts.* Urbana, IL: National Council of Teachers of English.

Smith, M. A., & Murphy, S. (1992). "Could you please come and do portfolio assessment for us?" *The NWP/CSW Quarterly, 14* (1), 14-17.

Swain, S. (in press). How portfolios empower process. In T. Newkirk (Ed.), *Workshop 5,* Portsmouth, NH: Heinemann

Taylor, D. (1990). Teaching without testing: Assessing the complexity of children's literacy learning. *English Education, 22* (1), 4-74.

Tierney, R. (in press). Testing higher order thinking. In Purves, A. (Ed.) *Encyclopedia of English studies and language arts.* Urbana, IL: National Council of Teachers of English.

Valencia, S. (1990). A portfolio approach to classroom reading assessment: The whys, whats, and hows. *The Reading Teacher, 43* (4), 338-340.

Vavrus. L. (1990). Put portfolios to the test. *Instructor, 100* (1), 48-53.

Wiggins, G. (1992). Creating tests worth taking. *Educational Leadership, 49* (8), 26-33.

Wiggins, G. (1989). Teaching to the (authentic) test. *Educational Leadership, 46* (7), 41-47.

Wiggins, G. (1989). A true test: Toward more authentic and equitable assessment. *Phi Delta Kappan, 70* (9), 703-713.

Wolf, D. P. (1989). Portfolio assessment: Sampling student work. *Educational Leadership, 46* (7), 35-39.

Wolf, D. P. (1987, December/1988, January). Opening up assessment. *Educational Leadership, 45* (4), 24-29.

Wolf, D., Bixby, J., Glenn, J., III, & Gardner, H. (1991). To use their minds well: Investigating new forms of student assessment. *Review of Research in Education, 17*, 31-74.

Wolf, D. P., LeMahieu, P. G., & Eresh, J. (1992). Good measure: Assessment as a tool for educational reform. *Educational Leadership, 49* (8), 8-13.

Newsletters

Assessment Matters. California Assessment Collaborative. 730 Harrison Street, San Francisco, CA 94107.

Portfolio Assessment Newsletter. Five Centerpoint Drive, Suite 100, Lake Oswego, OR 97035

Portfolio News. University of California, San Diego, Teacher Education Program, 9500 Gilman Drive, La Jolla, CA 92093-0070

Portfolio News-Letter. English Department, University of North Carolina at Charlotte, Charlotte, NC 28223

The Watershed—Science Portfolio. California Learning Assessment System, California Department of Education, P.O. Box 944272, Sacramento, CA 94244-2720